Bill Cullen was born in Dul... ...er city slums of Dublin's Sumn... ...b in a Dublin Ford car dealership and by 1964 – still only ... two – had been appointed director general of the dealership. In 1986 he took over the troubled Renault car distribution franchise and turned it into a success. Bill Cullen is a director of the Irish Youth Foundation. In 1998 he was a recipient of the Lord Mayor's Award for his work with the disadvantaged young people of Dublin and the inaugural Princess Grace Kelly Humanitarian Award in 2004 for his work with children.

Praise for *Golden Apples*:

'Can Bill Cullen's book change the lives of those who read it? For my money, the answer is yes . . . a charming, down-to-earth guide to getting on in life.'

Feargal Quinn, *Irish Times Weekend Review*

'Laced with anecdotes and written in simple and compelling prose. He is a natural writer.'

Sunday Independent, Dublin

'A self-help book with that little something special which Cullen brings to all his projects . . . He is an inspiration.'

Irish World

'A distillation of his mother's homespun utterances, and those of his more philosophical grandmother, with business and fitness principles of his own soldered on. If there is a "secret" to his success, it seems to be no more complicated than having seized opportunities to impress and been prepared to work harder, faster and for longer than anyone else.'

Daily Telegraph

'A wonderfully inspiring story.'

Liverpool Daily Post

Also by Bill Cullen

It's A Long Way From Penny Apples

GOLDEN APPLES:
Six Simple Steps to Success

BILL CULLEN

HODDER

Copyright © 2005 by Bill Cullen

First published in Great Britain in 2005 by Hodder and Stoughton
A division of Hodder Headline

A Hodder paperback

8

A CIP catalogue record for this title is
available from the British Library

ISBN 978-0-340-83898-3

Typeset in New Baskerville by Hewer Text Ltd, Edinburgh
Printed and bound by Clays Ltd, St Ives plc

Hodder Headline's policy is to use papers that are natural, renewable
and recyclable products and made from wood grown in sustainable forests.
The logging and manufacturing processes are expected to conform
to the environmental regulations of the country of origin

Hodder and Stoughton Ltd
A division of Hodder Headline
338 Euston Road
London NW1 3BH

The silver apples of the moon
The golden apples of the sun

W.B. YEATS: The Song Of Wandering Aengus

THE MA, MOLLY DARCY, THE DA

We all owe a huge debt of gratitude to our parents. For me and my brothers and sisters, our parents were extra special. Raising fourteen children in the tenement slums of Dublin in the '40s wasn't easy.

The Da diligently taught us his army habits of doing things right. The Ma taught us to do the right thing and do them right now, as she worked around the clock to support the needs of her ever-growing family. They made so many sacrifices to create a better life for their children.

Our grandmother, Molly Darcy, who lived for 100 years,

was always there to give a sense of peace and wisdom to the frantic pace of life in Dublin's teeming inner-city of that time. She gave me the self-confidence, the values, and the beliefs of her Celtic Warriors.

These three wonderful people developed and nurtured my business skills as a street-seller and it is thanks to them that I evolved my **Six Simple Steps to Success**.

Bill Cullen
January 2005
Lakes of Killarney

CONTENTS

FOREWORD

SIR RICHARD BRANSON
Chairman of Virgin Group & Companies

Bill Cullen's memoir, *It's A Long Way From Penny Apples*, told the story of his extraordinary journey from rags to riches. It's also a tribute to his mother, Mary Cullen. This proud woman had no formal education but her common sense, determination and positive attitude saw her succeed in raising her large family in the Dublin slums. 'I want to give you the independence to stand on your own feet.'

Bill Cullen got a wonderful training as a fruit seller on the streets, learning to buy, and to negotiate, while he was still only a child. He was a child who grew into a high achiever. Thanks to his street mentoring he now stands as one of Ireland's peak performers in Ireland's *Top 50 Rich List*.

And Bill has never forgotten where he came from. As President of the Irish Youth Foundation he has led the fundraising of forty million dollars for kids' charities in-cluding a one million dollar covenant from his *Penny Apples* book. Bill was awarded the inaugural Princess Grace Kelly Humanitarian Award in 2004 for his work with children.

This new book, *Golden Apples*, shows how he has ingrained the habits of success into his everyday life. *Six Simple Steps To Success* is the platform for his achievements. Bill explains, in his own easy style, how anyone can adopt his philosophy with immediate results in improving their career, their business and their personal life.

This book will have a hugely positive impact on everyone who reads it.

Richard Branson
London. January 2005

ENDORSEMENT FOR
GOLDEN APPLES

DR MICHAEL SMURFIT,
Chairman, the Jefferson Smurfit Group Plc

Golden Apples is a book to cherish, a roadmap to success from one of Ireland's greatest achievers.

Bill Cullen started life as one of fourteen kids in the tenement slums of Dublin. He now shows us the core values and actions that underpinned his success. He shares the wise mentoring he received from his parents. The nurturing and confidence building he got from his wonderful grandmother, Molly Darcy. The life experiences he got from an early age as a street-seller where he learned his business basics the hard way.

Golden Apples is a goldmine; you can take a nugget from it every day for the rest of your life. A book that gives you a **simple plan** to revitalise your life. Bill will inspire you to get up off your butt and realise that you can create your own future, and he gives you the tools to achieve your success.

Golden Apples will make you sit up and live your life to the full. It will really show you how to make your dreams come true. It's a great book and I enjoyed every minute of it.

Michael Smurfit
December 2004

AUTHOR'S NOTE

The success of my *Penny Apples* book made me realise just how much I owed to so many people who had helped and mentored me: parents, brothers, sisters, teachers, friends and relatives.

That review of my life brought home to me how the street selling experiences I had with my mother gave me a superb basic training in business skills. There is no school, no college, no university in the world that can replicate the real life experience of negotiating, of buying and selling to make a profit. Knowing at every moment that you are risking your mother's nest egg concentrates the mind. How can a schoolteacher explain the feelings of a twelve-year-old bankrupt, and the emotions I felt watching my pigs drowning in the floods of a Dublin river in 1954? Learning that the only failure is not to try. Better still, learning that the so-called failures are the best experiences for moulding future achievements!

It was in those tough days that I developed the habits of

success, building the mental and physical strength to win. Acquiring the common sense and confidence that's at the core of all business decisions and the instinct to do the right thing at the right time.

While writing my *Penny Apples* memories, I relived those experiences, and it became clear to me that there were specific attributes that developed and evolved into my platform for Lifetime Success. Selling the penny apples on the streets of Dublin shaped my business acumen and formulated the *Golden Apples* philosophies that have become part of my psyche.

So, my thanks to my street selling professors: the Ma, our ever caring, ever busy, mother; my grandmother Molly Darcy, who lived to 100 years old and had the wisdom of the ages. My Da who taught me to measure twice and cut once. My sister Vera who taught me the meaning of integrity. She was my minder as a kid, and is now minder to her own ten kids and six grandchildren. She was at my side through those early days.

The late Billy Wallace Snr., of Walden Ford, who gave me my first real opportunity to achieve. Brendan Hession, probably the best car salesman in Ireland, who taught me the secrets of motor trade profitability – when you buy right it's easy to sell right.

Paddy Hayes, CEO of Ford Motor Company and Waterford Crystal, who in both capacities was a great supporter. All my colleagues in Renault Ireland who have stood shoulder to shoulder with me in raising the flag so proudly, and particularly Jerr Nolan for his unwavering support when times get rough.

A big hug to my Jackie whose insight and marketing brilliance are always an inspiration to me.

To my assistant Christine a special thanks for all her help and early hours of extra-curricular activities.

To my daughters, Anita and Hilary, and my grandsons, Callum and Aidan. I hope my writings will be a valuable part of my legacy to them.

To Ivor Kenny a special thank you for his advice on the manuscript.

Finally, thanks to Sue Fletcher and all her team at Hodder & Stoughton who have supported my publications, and to Sheila Crowley who guided my route in the bookselling business.

Bill Cullen

1

THE TOUGH OLD DAYS

They called the 'thirties, 'forties and 'fifties 'good ould days'
and the 'rare oul times'. As a fella who experienced those
times, growing up in the tenement slums of Dublin, I'd say
that a more accurate description would be the 'tough old
days'. Those times were sometimes rare, sometimes good
but always, always tough.

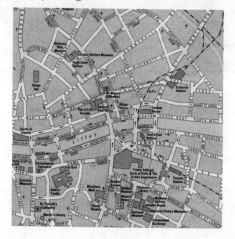

The Irish Free State was formed in 1922 when the English armed forces left our shores after eight hundred years of suppression and persecution. It should have been a time to celebrate our freedom, but no, it was a civil war we had instead, with brother fighting brother and friend killing friend.

When the country eventually settled down to self-rule it was a sad and sorry state we were in. The land was still owned

Bill's mother (Mary Darcy) with his sisters Rita and Betty in matching frocks, baby sister Vera and neighbour's children at the rear of the Summerhill tenements in 1940

by the English landlords and most businesses were controlled by the aristocracy. While the merchant princes of Ireland were of English descent, the vast majority of the native Irish people were rural peasants or working-class labourers with little or no work for them. From the 1920s to the 1980s the young people of Ireland had little option but to emigrate. To England and America they went to join with relatives and friends in the search for a job and the prosperity that work brings.

Dublin was one of the most gracious of European cities, with beauty spots like St Stephen's Green, O'Connell Street, Merrion and Fitzwilliam Squares, and the Phoenix Park, but it was easy to find the rundown tenement slums. On the Southside, the Liberties and the Coombe were the black spots. But on the Northside the tenement slums were only a stone's throw from the city centre. Gardiner Street, Summerhill, Sean MacDermott Street, Montgomery Street, Sheriff Street were described as 'rabbit warrens of despair', with the people still living in semi-derelict buildings that had been listed as uninhabitable as far back as 1890.

These tenements were four-storey-over-basement houses with two rooms on each floor. They had dilapidated roofs and windows that the rain poured through. No heat except the turf fire, no electricity – it was candles or oil lamps; no plumbed water – you brought it up the stairs in buckets from the tap in the backyard. No toilets – there was one tin-roofed shed in the backyard, shared by all the families.

The tenants lived one family to a room, so there could be eight to ten families in each house – Catholic families with a ban on contraception, so most mothers had a new baby every year. One single house had 130 people living in it and one of the mothers had twenty-two children. 'Irish twins' were common: one baby born at each end of the same year in separate pregnancies.

These conditions were poor and miserable but my parents didn't let us do misery. 'There will be no moaning or whinging in this house' was my mother's mantra. 'Once we have our health and the strength to work we'll always have bread on the table.'

Mary Darcy was my mother's name before she married Billy Cullen. She had finished school at seven years old to go selling apples and fish on the streets of Dublin with her mother Molly Darcy. It was only in recent days that I learned how my mother had been ineligible to take her Holy Confirmation, the Catholic celebration of adulthood, our bar mitzvah. As her schoolteacher said, 'She had missed school, didn't know her Catholic catechism, had no religious knowledge.' Harsh words. So she wasn't fit to go before the Archbishop with her former school friends to be confirmed into the Catholic fraternity. In fact she was now excommunicated from the Catholic religion.

Although the Ma did miss the Confirmation Day, Molly Darcy was a determined woman and down she went to the Pro-cathedral and appealed to the parish priest.

Molly Darcy had no schooling at all herself but she got her Mass and Holy Communion every day at six o'clock in the morning, before she went in to the markets, and her daughter Mary was always with her. Every evening they were in the church to thank God for a good day on the street. Even on the bad days they prayed that tomorrow would be better.

'This daughter of mine knows more about religion than some of your priests. She can recite the Mass in Latin off by heart, and like meself she can read this prayer book on the Life of Saint Ignatius Loyola who she knows like a brother.'

The priest was so impressed by this raw fervent Christian woman that he did make a special case.

So young Mary Darcy and her pal Alice Lindsay, who had left school with Mary, were invited to the Bishop's Palace in Drumcondra to be confirmed in the private chapel by Archbishop Welch himself. She borrowed the white confirmation dress and veil from her street-selling pal Lena Redmond and up they went on Uncle Bob's horse and cart to the Palace. Molly and Uncle Bob witnessed the Confirmation and the little group had tea and scones with the Archbishop after the ceremony. A day to remember, thanks to the quiet determination of Molly Darcy, who lived up to her reputation of never taking 'no' for an answer.

So it's easy to see where the Ma got her positive attitude from: the acorn never falls far from the tree. It was this positive attitude that cascaded down to her children where I, as the oldest boy in the family, took on the mantle of her *aide-de-camp*. For me it was also Mass every morning at six o'clock before we headed off to the Fruit Markets to buy the day's produce. Earlier still on Fridays, when Molly Darcy and I had to get the train to Howth harbour to meet the trawlers coming in to the quayside and buying the glistening slippery herring and mackerel. It was the selling of the fish, the fruit, the vegetables and the flowers that kept the family alive in those tough times. With no work for the men, the women of Ireland became the backbone of their families and of the nation.

So in those miserable conditions of the Summerhill tenements there were many families who overcame the deprivation with a strong Christian outlook. It really was a caring community, a sharing community. When it rained you took in the neighbour's washing off the clothesline as well as your own. When a mother went into the maternity hospital, the neighbouring women moved in to look after the family. Get himself out to work with a breakfast in his belly, make sure the kids did their homework and washed themselves and said their prayers. It was a wide extended family that took care of each other. We weren't poor at all, we just had no money – but we did have values that counted for much more.

So young Bill Cullen became a street seller in his own right, starting with the apples and moving up to the flowers. I learned from the flower-selling two priceless lessons. First, that it's all about location, location, location. Where is the best place to sell flowers? Outside the maternity hospital. The visiting father can't resist buying a bunch of flowers to bring to the mother with her new baby. Second, the elasticity of price. When that guy is running in late, he doesn't care how much the flowers cost, you can keep the change.

Newspapers were a basic everyday activity. You didn't need money – you got a few dozen newspapers on sale or return and out you went on the street selling and just paid for what you sold and kept the profit. In newspapers, the money was in volume – the bigger the number you sold the bigger the percentage profit you got. It was about energy too! Running to get to the factories in time to catch the workers at the afternoon tea break, get to the railway station as the express train from Cork arrived. Go where the people are in big numbers, and move as they move. That's why our biggest earner was always the ball games at Croke Park, our national stadium that held 100,000 fans.

We were energised on the big ball-game days. Up at the

crack of dawn to sell the Sunday newspapers outside the churches. Selling the rosettes for the fans to show their colours. Learning about the USP – the unique selling proposition, as we clipped the pictures of the star players from the unsold newspapers (which we got for free) and pasted the photo on our rosettes. The fans would queue up to buy our rosettes and pay more for the added value. The brothers and sisters sold fruit outside the stadium. As the kick-off time neared we backed closer to the stadium and took the empty wooden fruit boxes inside. On the terraces we sold these boxes for the small guys to stand on to see the game. With the stadium full we diverted up to the railway line behind the ground where we had a ladder to let the disappointed fans go up to sit on the long railway wall. A hundred and twenty extra spectators at a fee of half the ticket price! Ancillary activities.

During the game we moved through the crowd, still selling apples and oranges and pears, and after the match we collected the shattered remains of our wooden fruit boxes, which we sold as fire-kindle the following week. A non-stop sixteen-hour day for the family that was worth six months of the Da's pay for the Ma.

In December, we sold toys on the streets. In those cold rainy days we stood on the streets doing the spiel: 'Get yer bells, balls, balloons, and tinsel. Get yer monkey on the stick, yer Mickey Mouse, yer Donald Duck and yer Pinachiooooo.' My biggest coup was dressing up the plain plastic dolls in a Judy Garland gingham dress and pigtails; the spiel was, 'Get yer Judy Garland, she's dropped in Over the Rainbow to brighten yer day.' We added more value to the dolls when we put the Marilyn Monroe blonde tresses on, with her white dress starched stiff over her head. Little did we know then, in 1955, that we had the template for the Barbie Doll empire in our hands.

When we sold cool water by the mugful from a bucket on the terraces at the football game and hot water on the beaches to make tea for the picnics, it was another empire-building template that farseeing entrepreneurs took to fruition. So you see, the acres of diamonds are in full view, in your own field, if you have the vision to see them, and the energy to work them.

All this time I was getting daily lessons from the Ma, who taught me how to buy right. How to evaluate the price of one box of oranges versus another. The packing date stamp let you compare the age of the oranges – there was no refund if you opened the box to find half the oranges rotten. It was *caveat emptor*, let the buyer beware, so you had to be on full alert all the time.

In the 'forties when food was rationed, the Ma invented tea bags. At the time tea was sold loose in packets and you made the tea by putting one or two spoonfuls into the boiling water in the teapot. That's why we had tea-strainers to catch the leaves so you could drink from a tea leaf-free cup of tea. With a scarcity of tea, the Ma made little bags from the muslin cloth she used for steaming the Christmas pudding. A little muslin bag, filled with three or four spoons of tea leaves, hung by a string at the gas-stove. Everyone got a turn dipping the tea bag into their cup of warm water until it turned brown and then passed the bag onto the next person around the table. Sometimes it lasted all week, by which time you had to squeeze the bag against the side of your cup to get any colour at all into your cuppa. The Ma sure cut down on tea costs – pity we didn't patent the muslin tea bag idea!

Selling the Fruit & Vegetables from the Wicker Carts

The Ma had her little tricks to give us a 'hard neck'. Whenever you were sent to the shops for groceries she would send you back to exchange an item. For no reason. 'Work it out yourself son,' she'd say, marking the item with a little dot. 'Just go on back to the shop and get an exchange.' So back you go.

'Mister O'Riordan, can I swap these sausages, the Ma says they're too pale she wants redder ones' or 'Missus O'Brien, this packet of tea – I got Barry's tea instead of Lyon's. Can you just change it for me?'

She taught us to be assertive from an early age, even as children taking on adults. A hard neck she called it but it was building self-confidence in us that was the bedrock for being proactive and positive in later life.

The Ma's lasting legacy was teaching me the two great secrets of being effective in life: *Identify the Most Important Thing You Have to Do* and then *Do It Right Now*. It's simple common sense that isn't very common. Every day she'd have me write out the list of things to do and then number them and then she'd say, 'Let's go and do number one.' I didn't know the meaning of prioritising back then but that's for sure what we were doing. A habit that's been ingrained in me ever since.

The Ma was a dynamic woman who slept only four hours a night as she coped with her children and a full-time job on the streets. She was always positive, determined, and energised and I was lucky to be so close to her that I absorbed her enthusiastic attitude.

The Da was an army man who brought discipline to his children. In those tough times, many of the young people in our neighbourhood got into trouble with the police and others took refuge from their problems by drinking. Well, the Da's first law was simple: 'There'll be none of my children drinking or smoking.'

I was lucky enough to get involved in gymnastics and football at a young age so I've never smoked and I didn't have an alcoholic drink until I was well into my thirties. There's no doubt that my energy was channelled at full-steam into outworking my colleagues and powering my way into the upper executive echelon by the time I was twenty-two years old.

My grandmother, Molly Darcy, had a huge impact on me as a kid. Her approach to life was simple, quiet, and yet so effective. Molly had always sold fruit and fish and second-hand clothes on the streets even before her husband, Sheriff Robert Darcy, who had been a bakery worker, died of ingesting flour in his lungs. Molly's style was very different from the Ma's. Where the Ma was a dynamic, go-go, all out action person, Molly was quiet and deliberate. She was very observant as befits someone whose favourite saying was, 'You got two eyes, two ears and one mouth for a very good reason.'

Molly knew everyone and everyone knew Molly. When a family approached her and the mother enquired, 'How much are the apples, Missus?'

The answer was usually a big smile with the words, 'And how are you today Mam, isn't it a lovely day?'

This got the answer, 'That it is, thank God.'

To which Molly would reply, 'And that we do every day, we thank Him for His blessings and our health.'

A short pause before Molly would venture, 'Do I recognise you Mam, are you Missus O'Brien from Inchicore?'

A quick response, 'Not at all, I'm Missus Corcoran from Kimmage.'

Molly was into play: 'And these are your three lovely children,' which brought a big smile from Missus Corcoran, with the kids a bit red-faced and shy until Molly continued, 'Would you like a lollipop?' and reached under the apples at the rear of the tray and brought out three red lollipops. Three hands reached out, three mouths opened and went sucking the lollipops as Molly looked at the mother with a big smile on her face. 'Sure and it's three beautiful children you have Missus Corcoran, now how many apples did you say you wanted?'

What an example of developing rapport and empathy, of exceeding the customer's expectations, and taking the focus off the price of your product! Molly Darcy was a great saleswoman who also took care of her customers, remembered their names for ever. Be it a year since they'd last come to her, she'd still have her little smile and 'How are ya now Missus Corcoran, I haven't seen ya since the rainy April last year, and how are your three lovely children? Here's some lollipops for them, can I give you a few of these lovely Pippin apples?'

Molly made sure she used a customer's name as often as possible and that's a people skill we should all learn. She had absolutely no formal education but she taught me all the secrets of selling.

A teacher, a mentor and above all a great motivator, Molly Darcy would tell us stories by the turf-fire. About her great Celtic heroes, Brian Boru, Finn MacCool, and CúCullen. 'And you have the warrior blood in your veins, son,' she would say to me, 'the blood of the greatest warrior to ever walk our lands. You are a descendant of the great CúCullen so you need never fear any man.'

As a young fella listening to Molly in the flickering glow of the turf-fire, I found this inspirational. I was a warrior, with the strength of my ancestors to achieve anything I set my mind to. Believe and you will succeed.

On the morning I headed off to my first real job as a fourteen-year-old messenger boy at Walden Ford I got my parting advice from Molly. 'No matter what they give you to do, do it better then anyone else ever did it before. If you've to clean windows then clean them so well they wouldn't know there was a window there at all. If you've to sweep floors sweep them so clean a king could eat his dinner off it. Do your best at everything, and keep a smile on your face.' So I went off to tackle the world with two of the most important attributes: great enthusiasm and a positive attitude.

That was almost fifty years ago and those years have been good to me. Although I had been expelled from school at thirteen years of age, I worked hard, went to night school, and was always lucky to be in the right place at the right time. Then again, do you make your own luck or isn't luck really opportunity meeting preparation? I can tell you that I have been blessed with success in achieving my goals. Today, at sixty-three years old, I have the health and strength of a forty year old because I work hard at staying fit. I have all the trappings of financial success, because when you work hard and effectively you will make money. As Molly Darcy told me 'When you do a lot more than you're paid to do, eventually you'll be paid a lot more for what you do.'

I don't care how old you are – twenty, or forty or sixty or even eighty, it's never too late to go and achieve those dreams you have. We don't believe in middle age in our house because we stay active and busy both mentally and physically. When I filled in my Keyman insurance form in 2004 I got a phone call from the broker.

'Mister Cullen there's a mistake on the form here. You've put your retirement date down for 2050; shouldn't that be 2005?' he said.

'No the year 2050 is correct,' I replied.

A long pause.

'But, Mister Cullen you would be a hundred and eight years old then.'

'Yes,' I replied, 'that should leave me about twenty-two years to have some real fun.'

Another long pause. Just before he hung up I heard him mutter.

'He's nuts.'

Well the fact is I don't ever intend to retire. I've got more exciting projects lining up every month. I've got lots more places to go and people to meet. It's not work, it's not chores, it's an enthusiasm for achieving with the God-given potential that we *all* have inside us.

You know what happens when you retire? You are on the slippery slope to old age. The garden, the golf course, the bingo, the bridge games, the TV. All okay for leisure activities as a rest from the day job but all time-wasting substitutes for the challenges and the joy of real life.

The joy of real life is about people. Meeting people, interacting with people, being involved in projects with other people. Staying mentally and physically active.

Japan has the highest life expectancy of any country in the world at an average of eighty-two years. Why? Diet is the first reason, mainly fish, vegetables and rice. Except for the Sumo wrestlers who eat to build weight, most Japanese people are slim, trim and lithe. You are what you eat!

Then it's mental attitude – they continue to live with the family. Old age is embraced, indeed it's revered. Molly Darcy passed away at one hundred years old with her great-great-grandchild on her lap, five generations around her. She lived in the extended family, with young people around her all her life. Participating in their play, listening to them, kept her up to speed on the new world they lived in. The Japanese have that tradition too.

They nurture their physical strength as well. Can you believe that in Japan they have physical fitness centres for the over 80s? Yes, you've got to be over eighty years of age to join the club where you exercise for an hour every day. And guess what? They go mountain climbing every weekend and some Japanese octogenarians have climbed Mount Kilimanjaro in Tanzania and it's 19,335.5 feet high (5,895 metres). Now that's a winner's way fitness plan for you, because the oldest member is 103 years of age and he is a regular attendee, enjoying life to the full.

That story reminds me of my own father who was a fit active man, a former soldier and champion boxer. Fit as a fiddle he was until the Ma died. At eighty years old he never got over that. From being a busy everyday Mass-goer, who walked his city of Dublin every day, talking to all the guys on the construction sites, bantering up and down the streets, the Ma's death knocked him for six. He just stayed at home looking at the television all day, snoozing in the chair, his lifetime partner no longer around to make sure he got on with life. He was soon moulded into the shape of his armchair. When he got to his feet his back was bent over, his knees were locked, his power walk reduced to a shuffle. It wasn't long before he took off too on the last journey after the Ma.

Youth is inside you, it's your mental attitude, and it's you who decides whether you are old or young. So make up your mind now that you can stay young by getting some projects to keep you busy. 'It's better to wear out than rust out' is what Molly used to say. No matter what age you are just take on board my **Six Simple Steps to Success** and you won't believe the difference it will make in your life.

I have achieved a lot in my sixty-three years on this earth. Believe me, with the help of God, I intend to achieve ten times more in the next forty years than I have in the past sixty. So don't ever think that it's too late, no matter what age you are. Don't ever think that life has passed you by or you are too old or it's too late to improve yourself and your situation. In the next six chapters of this book you will see how easy it can be to move yourself onwards and upwards. To improve your mental outlook and your attitude. To get better results in your career and your personal life. To get more and more people to help you. To be a happy, healthy high achiever. To make your dreams come true!

The next six chapters give you my APPLES philosophy.

Jackie was with me driving from O'Hare airport to Fitzpatrick's Hotel in Chicago, which is on one of the Great Lakes of America.

'Jackie, do you remember the names of the Five Great Lakes?' I asked.

'Yes, of course, I do. There's Michigan and there is, em, em, oh yes, it's Superior. That's two and the next is, em, em, I'll think of it now, and you can stop that silly grin, know-all, because I'll remember them.' Long pause, then, 'Yes, yes, it's Ontario.'

I nodded.

Another long pause. 'Okay, wise guy, what's the other two?'

'You know, it goes back to that great teacher I had in 1952, Brother Charlie Gallagher, the Christian Brother in St Canice's School in Dublin. He used acronyms and I never forget the Great Lakes because I just have to remember one word. Homes.

She smiled. 'Of course, the other two are Huron and Erie. What a terrific way to remember things.'

That conversation sparked a thought in me. I had just done the chapter outline of *Golden Apples* and realised that by using an acronym I could get every reader to remember forever my **Six Simple Steps to Success**. And I could use the produce that started my own selling career. That acronym is APPLES.

Using the word APPLES you can align the **Six Simple Steps to Success** like this:

A	is your warrior's **ATTITUDE** for achieving	**A**
P	is your dynamic **PLAN** of action	**P**
P	is your charismatic **PEOPLE** power	**P**
L	is the way you learn to be **LUCKY**	**L**
E	is your explosive **ENERGY** to excel	**E**
S	is your supercharged **SELLING** skills	**S**

Simple, isn't it? Get this APPLES acronym written across the inside of your forehead and never forget it. Have it on Post-Its at your desk, on your mirror, the dashboard of your car, inside your action planner. Ingrain the habits in your mind and practise the habits every day. This is the Golden Apples way to lifetime success.

2

A – DEVELOP A WARRIOR'S ATTITUDE FOR ACHIEVING

- Stay Positive
- I Am Terrific
- When The Going Gets Tough
- Believe You Can Achieve
- Dump The Negatives
- Worrying Doesn't Help
- You Are What You Think You Are
- The Sixty Second Review
- Have You A Hero?
- Just Imagine That
- You Gotta Have Lee-A-Roady
- The Darkest Hour
- You Are Number One
- Power Points

STAY POSITIVE

From my youngest days I've seen how my mother's courage and determination won through in the most despairing situations. She would never take no for an answer, as she struggled to raise her fourteen kids. She sold on the streets ten hours a day but was always around the house when we needed her. She lost two of her babies to the deprivation of the tenement slums but she hid her grief away and got on with the task of looking after the rest of us.

She was the champion of the community, leading the way to the highest levels in a cause for justice or defending our neighbours from eviction. Her attitude was always positive. If something needed to be done then she'd find a way to get it done. So from my mother I saw the power of a positive attitude as she took us from the slums to a house of our own. My grandmother, Molly Darcy, quietly reinforced my mother's dynamic attitude in her own calm supportive way.

My confidence was dented in 1956 when as a thirteen year old I was expelled from school. As the eldest boy in our family I had to help my mother sell her fruit and vegetables on the streets and the Christian Brothers were very unhappy with me missing two and three days a week from school. But I was a quick learner and read books into the night so I always got a top three score in the midterm exams. It was football that finished me. When a photo appeared in the newspaper showing me on the local under-fourteen soccer team, this was too much for a strict Irish Catholic school where the school sports were hurling and Gaelic football. Soccer was the sport of the English armed forces who had garrisoned Ireland for hundreds of years. So it was 'You're a traitor to your country and your school and expulsion it is for you me boyo!'

That year I wrote more than 700 job applications to the newspaper advertisements without getting a single reply because of our no-go address. I shared my frustration with a social worker in the boys' club who let me use his upmarket address. The first time we used it we got an immediate response. I got the job in a Ford Dealership and eight years later at age twenty-two I was General Manager of the company. Which shows if you stay positive and get people to help you, you can get the right result.

I AM TERRIFIC

To be a happy, healthy, high achiever you need to have a positive can-do attitude. So start with the fact that you are a unique, extraordinary creation of God with the potential to achieve your dreams. No matter where you are on the ladder of achievement you can improve in so many ways if you strengthen your positive attitude and believe passionately that you can and will succeed.

Let's start the day with an early morning confidence builder. Remember what Molly Darcy had me do – stand in front of that mirror and say:

> *I have warrior blood in my veins*
> *I need never fear any man*
> *I AM TERRIFIC*

Repeat those words 'I am terrific' twenty times before you leave the house every morning with a big smile on your face, ready to face the day because every day you can get out of bed is a great day. That's why I give my Smiley sticker to all the kids when I do a motivational visit to the schools. They each get a sticker to put on the mirror in the bathroom to remind them to do their 'I am terrific' mantra *every morning*.

Look forward to the challenges – they are opportunities for you to achieve and to develop your abilities. Problems are there to be solved and as Molly Darcy said, 'When God closes one door he always opens two more. But you have to keep your head up to spot them.' So I've always believed that for every problem there is a solution. Even if it means going over it, around it, or through it, we can and will overcome the obstacle. That's my warrior beliefs.

A positive attitude is paramount in solving problems. Every day in your life you meet problems and they can and will be solved. Look back at last year's diary and you'll remember you had lots of problems then too. And guess what? They have all been solved now, either solved or gone away.

So don't let problems get you down and don't worry about them. We are all born to be problem solvers and the quicker you tackle them, and the more mentally positive you are in your approach, the easier it is to reach the solution.

Visualisation plays a big part in confidence building and you will feel positive every time you repeat 'I am terrific' and see yourself as a warrior. Believe in your power to resolve all difficulties, expect that you will achieve the right result and you will. It's by sustaining your expectations to succeed that your success will happen. Nothing will beat you if you focus yourself on the problem and believe you can win.

Descartes, the French philosopher, said 'I think, therefore I am'. He confirmed that by visualisation you can use your mind to trick your body.

Look at the young elephants in India who are tied to a stake with a rope every night. They pull and pull but the rope doesn't break and the stake doesn't budge so in their minds these baby elephants become convinced they can't move if there is a rope around their necks. Forever after the adult elephants will not move if a rope, or even a light scarf, is placed around their neck. Mind over matter! The elephant, from past experience, believes he can't budge with a rope around his neck. So he stops trying. He believes he can't do it so he never will.

Many people are like these elephants. They are convinced by previous negative experiences that they should never try to do things. It is usually family influence, such as when children have to be protected and parents tell them, 'No, you can't swim in the river, the currents are too strong, it's dangerous.'

Worse still some parents get angry with kids and use threats like, 'No, don't climb trees, you could fall and kill yourself. Never let me catch you climbing trees or else!' So some kids will never dare to climb trees or learn to swim and as similar negative commands are given, they never want to try anything.

It doesn't have to be like that. We should generate positive thinking with children by saying, 'Yes, the river looks great, but let's get you some swimming lessons so you can swim in style', and 'Sure, tree climbing is exciting so let me get up there with you so we can climb to the top.'

Young people need encouragement and support to develop a positive can-do attitude, so they will believe they can achieve.

Henry Ford was right when he said:

*'If You Think You Can
Or You Can't – You're Right.'*

WHEN THE GOING GETS TOUGH

Street selling is a great training school for achievers because every day you have deadlines to meet and targets to reach. We got a week's credit on the fruit and vegetables we bought, so every Saturday was pay-up day. It was too bad if business was slow or the weather deterred shoppers, it was still pay-up and look happy. We were also selling perishable commodities in those pre-refrigeration days, so the goods became unsaleable very quickly.

We normally finished selling on the city centre streets at six o'clock but there were plenty of evenings when we had to keep going to nine o'clock to sell off the fruit. Up and down the cinema queues with a box of apples and oranges strung around your neck. 'Only a few left, get the last of the penny apples, three for two pence.' Few of us can resist a bargain. It was a case of getting rid of them at any price and once we put in the effort we always moved the stock. You developed determination and resilience and learned the value of cashflow.

The business of buying and selling cinema tickets was even more adventurous. Blackmarketeers, we were called, ticket touts and worse still 'scalpers'. For me those names are an insult to an honest and legitimate business, the very essence of entrepreneurship. The cinema tickets went on sale, and you took your place in the queue but you could only buy four tickets per person. So after the first four you reverted to the end of the queue to get another four. And so on it went until you had fifty tickets and had spent three or four hours queuing, usually in the rain.

Then you went on the street selling the tickets. Another few hours on the job. If the weather was too sunny the customers were at the beach, if the rain was too heavy they stayed home. If the film got a bad review they went else-where. You had to be real good to make a profit at that business and plenty of times we sold some tickets at half-price and even gave them away to friends for zilch. Donald Trump should test his apprentices at that game.

To think it's now classified as a criminal act is unbeliev-able. It's simply charging a premium for a service that the customers can't or won't do for themselves. Corporate event companies charge a 1000% premium for football tickets by throwing in a few drinks and a lunch to justify the savage premium. One law for the rich and another for the poor.

But I'll still say that ticket touting in the cinema world is at the leading edge of business skills, knowing what to buy, how many to buy, judging the film, guessing the weather, what premium to charge, knowing when to get out. Wow – it's a microcosm of on-the-floor stock trading, and you learn to make tough decisions.

BELIEVE YOU CAN ACHIEVE

By the time I was eighteen I had become a valuable cog in Walden Ford. I had gone to night school and took first place in the Business Diploma for Commerce. I did a shorthand and typing course which was a big laugh for a fella back forty years ago. But it gave me an opportunity to do after-hours typing for the boss when the secretaries had left, which got me noticed in the executive suite. Whenever anyone quit or was fired in any department I applied to take over the role until a replacement arrived. 'Can you handle the parts stock control job? Or the payroll clerk's job?' My reply was always 'Sure I can do it' and fit it in with my other duties by getting in early and working late into the evening. Of course, I didn't always know how to do the job but I learned fast. The word went around, 'If you need anything done get Bill Cullen.' And something else I got known for as well – smiling.

There's no doubt I was showered with positive thinking at home. We lived in miserable conditions all right but my mother would never let us do misery. 'No moaning or whinging in this house. Be thankful for the food on the table, the bed to sleep in and the clothes on your back. And once you have your health you have the best thing in life. So get a smile on yar face son and let's go meet the new day.' What the Ma didn't add but I had realised way back then, was that we had the loving care of wonderful parents and a great extended community who looked after each other.

Molly Darcy was my first great motivator. 'Your name is William,' she told me one night sitting by the turf-fire. 'And that name means "protector". You are also the oldest boy in the family so it'll be up to you to take care of your brothers and sisters. We all need you to grow up big and strong. That's why you must stay away from the smoking and drinking that drags people down. And play the football as much as you can to grow strong. But most important of all you've got to believe in yourself. You are a descendant of CúCullen, the chieftain and hero of the Red Branch Knights of Ulster. The bravest man ever to walk our lands – and his blood flows in your veins. His courage is in your heart. His strength is in your body. That's why you need never fear any man because you'll never meet a man better than yourself. So stand here son and look in the mirror. Always remember you are a warrior and you must stay strong to look after your family. Believe you are the best my son, because you are terrific.'

Wonderful words for a youngster to hear and I remember well on that cold winter night tingling with excitement. Vowing to myself that I would be strong and take on the challenges of life. I joined the boys' club, took up boxing, running, gymnastics, and football and built myself into a strong athlete. To this day I keep up my daily fitness-training schedule, which in my sixties I have compacted into less than thirty minutes a day.

But it's the mental strength I got from Molly Darcy that was so important, so inspiring. It motivated me to believe in myself, to realise that I didn't have to spend the rest of my life in the tenements. I could be an achiever just like my ancestor CúCullen the great chieftain warrior.

Looking back I now realise that I started to visualise myself as a Celtic warrior. Working hard to get fit and strong. Always being available to help the Ma on the street. Repeating to myself every morning 'I am terrific'.

My other coach was Tony Myles, our gymnastics instructor in the boys' club. Tony was an Olympian, small in stature like most good gymnasts. He had immense strength both physically and mentally. One evening in the middle of our gym class routine he gave a powerful lesson in positive thinking when he said to us, 'It's your mind that dictates your achievements. You can do anything you believe you can do.' Now as a twelve-year-old youngster back in 1954 in poor old Dublin this kind of talk was new to me. 'Let me show you,' said Myles, 'how your mind can set you free to do whatever you want to do.'

He got three of us to come out front and put a small ten-pound barbell in our right hands.

'Now I want you to lift that weight out sideways until it's at shoulder height, hold it a second, and return it down to your side. Okay, now continue lifting and let's see how many lifts you can do.'

He stood back as we continued lifting the weight. Nine repeats was the max.

'Now, my young friends,' said Myles, 'I want you up here every Monday night and I'll give a one pound note to anyone who can do fifty side lifts with that weight.'

Before I left Myles took me aside and gave me a lecture.

'You didn't try too hard on that one Cullen, so listen to me carefully,' he said with his face close to mine, glaring at me. 'You just gave up when you got a bit tired, no focus, no determination. So just watch me.'

He picked up the weight and started lifting and lowering it in a steady cadence, talking as he did it. 'I could do this all night because I believe it's not heavy, there's no weight, my hand is empty, this is simple.' Then he dropped the weight on the floor and slapped my face.

'You just go and do it you little gurrier,' he snapped at me and swaggered out the door.

A week later I did sixty-five lifts and took the money and that's when I absorbed the power of positive thinking. The mental strength, the belief that I could achieve the outcome I wanted.

I was in that gym with Tony Myles two nights a week for two hours a night for six years and it was there that I built the physical and mental strength that will sustain me for ever.

DUMP THE NEGATIVES

Knowing just how powerful a positive attitude has been in my life, I have always looked for it in people I work with. I look for enthusiastic, smiling, positive people, and over the years I've poached and headhunted and hired people with those attributes. That's why we have a great business today because of the positive people we have on board. People who want to learn, are proactive people, who want to achieve, want to get the job done, and are prepared to put the effort into achieving our objectives.

Why doesn't everyone have a strong positive attitude? Because many people are carrying all sorts of excess baggage that drags them down.

The baggage of worrying about mistakes they might make.
The baggage of past mistakes they did make.
The baggage of fear and anxiety about what might happen.
The baggage of missed opportunities.
The baggage of regrets for wrong decisions.
The baggage of failures they had.
The baggage of perceived injuries done by others.
The baggage of resentment for lack of support.
The baggage of envy for others' success.
The baggage of begrudging others' achievements.

Enough baggage to fill a truck and all of it a big heap of negative emotions. This kind of emotional stress will not just make you a loser, it could kill you.

That's right, negative thinking can poison your metabolism, ignite the dance of the cancer cells, and induce heart attacks and strokes.

So if you've got any of this excess baggage it's time to load the truck and dump it on the rubbish heap where it belongs. Give yourself a good shake and realise that you've got to let go of the past, you've got to forget and ignore the negatives. As for carrying a grudge, remember what Molly said: 'While you are sitting at home moaning the other guy is out dancing with the girls.'

Forget it and you go and enjoy life too. Get up on your two feet and start counting your blessings. One by one just scratch out your list of baggage, just let it go. Clear your head of those memories and get yourself into a positive state of mind.

WORRYING DOESN'T HELP

One fine Sunday evening I was sitting at the kitchen table doing school homework when Molly Darcy came to the open window. 'Now son, you're looking very worried there, is there something wrong?'

I grimaced a bit and replied, 'It's exam time next week Molly, and these science questions are a divil because I missed some of the classes.'

She looked at me for a while with her mystic smile on her face. 'Well thanks be to God I never had to bother with high faluting things like science. Are ya sure ya wouldn't like a walk with me up to Stephen's Green to feed the ducks. Only take an hour?' Silence. 'But sure if sitting here worrying about these things is of help to ya well you just sit there and worry away. I'm off to get some ice cream on me way to the ducks.' Her smiling face vanished from the window. It took me only ten seconds to get out the door after her and we had a great time in the park chasing butterflies, feeding the ducks, and eating the ice cream cones. And I passed the exams! It pays to take a break from the tension.

So, a saying to remember: 'If worrying is going to help let's all sit here and worry.' We must decide if there's anything we can do that will help solve the problem, then we do that. If not, let's keep our energy focused on the positives. Just as important, you must turn your back on the negatives and resolve to get rid of the bad habits. In particular:

Control your impatience with others
Don't lose your temper
Don't take criticism personally
Don't let yourself be frustrated
Don't be offended by other people's actions
Don't use sarcasm in your conversation
Don't 'take the hump' over perceived slights

The way to a positive attitude is through self-confidence, really believing you can do whatever it is that needs to be done. Yes, you might need to be shown how; and yes, you might need some help or support, but believe you can do it. The secret of success is to really believe that you can achieve and you will. You might make some mistakes but that's ok, that's a learning curve. The man who never made mistakes never made anything. Just be careful not to make the same mistake twice.

YOU ARE WHAT YOU THINK YOU ARE

Stress is the anxiety and mental pain that we suffer as we react to negative circumstances. Stress is a proven contributing factor to ulcers, heart attacks and cancer, so the mental pain becomes a physical ailment. The negative thoughts generate anxiety, causing stress which harms the body.

Negative thoughts have a negative impact on our bodies, so our thoughts clearly affect our bodies, and it's our thoughts that will have a positive or negative impact on our health, on our happiness, on our ability to achieve.

The secret of success is to stay thinking positive, always to look on the bright side of life. No matter what disaster happens to you there's always millions of people who are worse off than you will ever be. If you stay thinking positively you will generate the power to overcome any crisis and become stronger from the experience.

If you allow negative thoughts to make you unhappy, distressed and physically ill, that's your own responsibility. It's your choice: by allowing negative thoughts to invade your mind, you are deciding to opt out of living a successful life!

THE SIXTY SECOND REVIEW

The very first thing to realise about a positive attitude is how important your self-image is. How do you feel about your appearance and how do you want other people to perceive you? What do people see when they look at you?

Well, the fact is we often make up our mind in one minute about someone we're meeting for the first time. So you should always look your best. No matter whether it's work or play always check that your appearance is neat and smart. It doesn't have to cost money to look your best but it does take a bit of time and attention.

My Da was a trained army man and forever lived by their standards of clean smart appearance. So even in the tenements where we had only the bucket of water and a basin, you scrubbed every day, stripped to the waist under the tap in the backyard. Hair washed and combed. Shoes cleaned the army way with spit and polish. Trousers always folded and put on a newspaper under the mattress every night. With six in the bed the crease was razor sharp next morning! But most important of all was the power walk, army style. The Da didn't just walk down the street, he marched, and we had to fall in and do the same.

'You never leave the house son, without a smile on your face, a spring in your step and your head held high.'

It was left, right, left, right in brisk cadence with arms swinging smartly as you went along.

'Always walk as if you're on a mission, something important to do. And that's easy because your mother always has her list of jobs for you to do.'

HAVE YOU A HERO?

I've always had heroes, icons who inspired me to achieve more, peak performers who have made it happen, won the gold. Of course, my first hero was CúCullen the legendary figure from Irish mythology. As a boy named Setanta he strayed on to the land of an important man called Cullen and was set upon by the guarding hound. In defending himself the youngster used his camawn – a wooden hurley stick – to strike a stone which hit the hound on the head and killed him. His punishment was to be detained for twelve months as Cullen's security guard until a new hound was found and trained for the task. He was known ever after as Cúcullen (Cú is Gaelic for hound). The Hound of Cullen.

I absorbed the tales of CúCullen's deeds. How he became the leader of the warrior clan the Red Branch Knights of Ulster, his feats of bravery and valour in the battles with Queen Maeve of Connaught. How he was mortally wounded by Ferdia in the struggle over the Brown Bull of Cooley. He tied himself to a tree stump and the army on the other side of the river were afraid to advance against this lone warrior so awesome was his reputation. He was dead for three days before a raven dared land on his shoulder and plucked out his eye, which confirmed he was dead, and the army gave him a king's burial before dispersing in respect. Is it any wonder this great warrior was my hero!

I have also been inspired by the never say die determination of Winston Churchill, the genius and innovation of Henry Ford and Andrew Carnegie, the courage and bravery of Nelson Mandela, the resolve and focus of Muhammad Ali.

And it's not just world renowned heroes that can inspire you. I also have my first business mentors, Bill Lambert and Michael Cole, my gymnastics instructor, Tony Myles, my motor industry consultant, Ron Sewell and our two great Irish business icons Tony O'Reilly and Michael Smurfit. Some mentors are close enough to mould and guide you.

Others are achievers whose deeds you admire and this strengthens your own resolve to succeed.

Warriors don't have to be men. My mother was a dynamic warrior who raised her family of fourteen children in the tenement slums, losing two babies to the miserable conditions. She sold fruit on the streets to supplement the Da's meagre income and lived her life dedicated to her family, sleeping only three or four hours a night. In so many ways she remains the wind beneath my wings.

Lance Armstrong

In these new millennium years I have two modern-day warriors. The first one is Lance Armstrong, the king of road cycling. Lance was already a cycling hero when he was struck down with cancer. After intensive chemotherapy he was left scarred physically and emotionally but he made a miraculous recovery and returned to his cycling career to win the sport's highest prize – the Tour de France – in 1999 and has gone on to win the Tour a record-breaking six times. This man is a unique warrior whose determination and courage is inspirational. He has now founded the Lance Armstrong Foundation to play a pivotal role in the fight against cancer.

Kelly Holmes 800 & 1500 Metre Gold Medal

My other modern-day warrior is Kelly Holmes, the English athlete who achieved a historic double gold victory in the Athens Olympics for the Women's 800 and 1500 metres. Kelly Holmes was a career soldier as a physical training instructor in the British Army. She finished fourth in the Atlanta Olympics in 1996, suffering from a nagging stress fracture. In the 1997 World Championships a ruptured Achilles tendon ruined her chances. She took time out to go to Africa, determined to rebuild her strength. Then she returned to Athens for the double gold she had worked so hard to achieve. Her lean sculpted body powered down the finishing stretch leaving everyone gasping at an astonishing achievement. Determination, raw courage and focus have proved again to be priceless assets of a warrior striving to achieve.

JUST IMAGINE THAT

Let's learn how to have positive visualisation that will give us positive expectations and positive results. Visualising is one of the strongest motivators for achieving.

Try this next time you have a spare ten minutes. Sit down quietly in an armchair, close your eyes and breathe deeply into your belly. Imagine your dream has come true, and that you are driving your Bentley Continental GT into your mansion driveway, past the massive Bell 430 helicopter

Bill and the helicopter

37

resting on the helipad. Sense the feel of the car's soft cream leather. The crunching of the stone pebbles under the wheels, the purr of the exhaust. The swish of the tyres as you swing the Bentley in front of the massive stone staircase at the entrance door of your home. You step out of the car and shut the door with its prestigious clunk and feel the adrenalin pumping into your system.

Open your eyes and you feel exuberant. The endorphins go rushing around your metabolism and you want to move fast to get some of your projects up to speed.

Visualisation works in other parts of your life. If you want to lose weight you have to control your food intake and get an exercise routine as you will see in detail later on. But you should also use mind pictures. Sit down again in a comfortable armchair in a quiet place and breathe through your belly not your chest. Imagine yourself at your ideal weight – say twenty-five pounds lighter. Wearing a suit four sizes smaller than today. Looking slim and trim and fit. Laughing and joking with your friends. You will feel the happy chappies coursing through your body.

Log the scene into your mental computer to recall every time you finish your fitness routine and it will speed up your weight loss plan.

Go one better and buy the new smaller suit, put it in the wardrobe and look at it every morning as you get closer and closer to the day you fit into it comfortably. Visualisation works.

Whatever your own personal dream is, visualise yourself celebrating its achievement and log the scene into your memory, available for you to recall anytime you sit down and close your eyes. Ten minutes of relaxing tranquillity that revives your energy and puts a positive focus on your activities. Then go tackle the steps of your plan of action that we will build with you later, and you will move closer to achieving your dream.

YOU GOTTA HAVE LEE-A-ROADY

The word *entrepreneur* has a lovely ring to it. Like all French words it has a sophistication and a lot of chic that belies its real meaning – risk-taking. When you want to succeed in life and achieve your objectives you have to take risks. Sometimes you'll fail and that's part of learning to succeed. But sometimes you can turn a losing situation into a win by having the determination, the courage, the fighting spirit to make it happen, to win.

My first vivid recollection of my mother's fighting spirit was in the tenement slums back in 1948. Let me tell you this story, which I first wrote in *Penny Apples*. I was six years old. In the story I'm called Liam – my family name – because my Da was Bill then. The Ma had come home early from her apple-selling on the street and was having a rest when we heard a shout.

'Avicshun! Avicshun! The Corpo are here for Missus Walsh! It's an avicshun!'

'Did I hear "avicshun"?' the Ma asked slowly.

Rita nodded just as the roar went up again: 'Avicshun! Avicshun! It's the Corpo for Missus Walsh.' With that, there was a loud bang of a door hitting the wall, and the tramp of hobnailed boots on the stone hall.

Mary's face flushed red and she stood up, with anger in her eyes. 'Give me that poker, Rita,' she said, 'and Liam,

39

you get that sweeping brush and come with me. You girls mind the little ones.' There was a pause as she retied her white apron around her swollen tummy and then took the poker and waved for Liam to follow her.

'I don't believe this,' she said. 'It can't be an avicshun in this day and age, in this kip of a house.' She opened the door and then leaned back to dip her fingers in the holy-water font and blessed herself and sprinkled some water on her son. There were roars and screams coming up the stairs from Missus Walsh's room at the back of the hall. 'Let's go,' she said and down the stairs she went, with Liam behind her.

The Corporation had taken over the tenements years before from the profiteering landlords who had evicted tenants left, right and centre for not paying their rent. But the Corpo had a more charitable outlook and evictions were now seldom seen. Only one had happened in the last twelve months: that had been at the top end of Summer-hill, and the ould fella was moving on anyway. It was still a fearful sight to see the Corpo men throw every piece of his belongings out onto the footpath and leave him sitting there in the rain while they boarded up the doors and windows of the room. His brother arrived later that night with a horse and cart. They loaded up his bits and bobs and off they went, never to be heard of again.

When Mary turned the corner of the stairs, she saw three Corpo lads in the hall, with Missus Walsh's table and chairs already being handed out from man to man. Some children were standing barefoot in the hall crying and she could hear Missus Walsh's voice from the room pleading tearfully: 'No, no, don't throw us out.'

Mary let out a roar – 'What's going on here, ya bowsies!'

– and she smashed the poker on the banisters with a loud crash that brought the men to a halt.

'Who's in charge here?' she shouted, and out from the room came a big, red-faced man, followed by Mister Sutton the rent collector. 'I'm in charge here, missus,' said the big man, in a country accent, 'now you just buzz off and mind your business. This is an official Corporation eviction, and you'll be in the clink if you're not careful.'

Mary gave the banister another bang with the poker. 'Well, aren't you the big brave culchie now, threatening women and children, sneaking in here when our men are out working to pay your rent? If it's trouble you want, you've come to the right place and I'm telling ya to leave Missus Walsh's things alone or you'll have me to deal with,' she shouted without taking a breath.

'And as for you, Mister Sutton, come out from hiding behind that culchie and speak up for yourself. Don't you know Mister Walsh was in hospital for a few months with the kidney stones. And he's back working now and they'll clear off the arrears. Don't ya know all that and why are ya here with these latchicos doing your dirty work?'

Mister Sutton just blinked behind his glasses as the big man did the answering. 'Listen, woman, it's none of your business. He's had plenty of warnings. When any tenant falls behind by more than six months' rent, it's out. That's the policy and there's no discussion.'

Turning to his men, he said, 'Right, me lads, let's get on with the job,' but before they could move Mary smashed the banister again with the poker.

'So that's the policy is it, now? Let's throw the sick man and his family out on the street is the policy, because they owe the Corpo a few lousy pounds. Let's get a big brave culchie up from Cork with his pals to dump them on the road. Sure they're well used to this job. Didn't some of ya help the English landlords during the famine days. Turncoats and informers ya are, who take on only the women and children. We'll leave the room there empty and put Missus Walsh out in the rain. Well that's the policy we had when the Brits were here, and many's the brave Irishman's blood was spilt to get them out and change that policy. Is this what Michael Collins fought for? Of course, he was a great man from Cork and he was shot in the back by one of his own. The like of you. Let me tell you this, me boyo – the first man that moves a stick of furniture out of this hall will get my poker over his head.'

What a tirade. The big Corkman was kicking the wall, saying, 'Feck ya! Feck ya! Feck ya!' Mary Darcy stood halfway up the stairs in her white apron, heavily pregnant, waving the poker, her face flushed with anger. Her young son stood beside her, with a sweeping brush held across his chest.

Mary came down the stairs into the hall and took a chair from one of the men, without resistance. 'Now, Mister Sutton,' she said, 'why don't you get these men out of here and let's see how we can clear off Missus Walsh's arrears. Sure I've two pounds here in me pocket. Wouldn't that be a better thing to do than have some of these culchies in hospital.'

The big man was livid with temper at the insults that had been heaped on him. He would have killed any man who used those words to him, but he was helpless and frustrated when faced with a pregnant woman.

The rent collector broke the tension. 'Well, are you saying, Missus Cullen, that we can have the arrears paid?' he asked.

'Of course I'm saying the arrears will be paid, Mister Sutton,' she replied. 'Get rid of these boyos and we'll sit down on these chairs and work everything out.'

'Right then,' said Mister Sutton, turning to the big man. 'You go on back to the office, Shamus, and I'll sort this out.'

The big man kicked the wall in frustration. 'Bejaysus, I'll go back to no feckin' office,' he said. 'I'll go down to Conway's pub and you'll meet us there to pay us for our day's work, so you will.' And down the hall he went, with the sparks flying from his hobnailed boots. The other men put down the furniture and trailed out after him.

'Bring that stuff in now, Liam,' said the Ma, 'and why don't you put the teapot on, Missus Walsh. I'm sure Mister Sutton could do with a cuppa tea while we talk business.' Twenty minutes later, Mister Sutton left, with the promise of six shillings a week payment off the arrears as well as the rent from next week on. Missus Walsh didn't know where she'd get the extra money from. 'Don't worry about that, Missus Walsh. We've won the haggle today, and we can win it again if need be,' said Mary, as she left to go back upstairs.

But as she sipped her tea, she grimaced and said, 'Liam, run down and tell Mother Darcy to come up here quick, and Vera, will you put that big pot of water on the stove.'

That evening, Carmel was born in the tenement room. The children had all been hooshed down to stay in Molly's. When they trooped back for bed, Mary was sitting up with the new baby and her husband Billy was there beside her. Mother Darcy was having a mug of shell cocoa; she had a proud look on her face and her sleeves were still rolled up. 'Mother Darcy brought the new baby up from the chapel in her shopping bag,' was the story Rita gave.

So you see, my mother was a hero in our neighbourhood. She was always ready to help – if you want something done, ask a busy person. But that story shows the courage and determination she had in her approach to every situation. An Irish word for courage is lee-a-roady and its technical translation is 'balls'. I've always said that my mother had more lee-a-roady than any man I have ever met!

THE DARKEST HOUR

We were always up against deadlines on the street. Usually it was bills to be paid. Pay for the fruit, pay for the rent, pay to get the Da's suit out of the pawnshop for Sunday Mass, pay for clothes and shoes for the kids, for food, and so on. Anyone who has had to live on a tight budget knows the feeling, but remember, we had fourteen mouths to feed.

Somehow the Ma always got us through those tough days. Many times she'd push it away for a while, by getting help from a neighbour, by soft-soaping a creditor, by calling in a favour, and sometimes by doing without. She would never turn to the moneylenders who soaked the poor people of our neighbourhood. Borrow £50 and pay £1 a week interest until you could repay the whole £50 in one lump. Some poor women would be paying the £1 a week for the rest of their lives.

Working with the Ma I learned that a determined positive attitude always brought the right result. In the toughest of situations she kept a brave face and kept all the balls in the air. She was practical and economical with the hard-earned cash, going around four or five grocery stores buying the different loss leaders from each of them. A lot of walking but a lot of money saved too.

Another of her tactics for cost cutting was taking the bulbs out of the bedroom at night. If any of us wanted to read in bed we saved to buy our own torch. That cut down on the electricity bill which otherwise went haywire because someone always fell asleep reading and left the light on all night. If you wanted to read you paid for your own light.

These practicalities sound like penny-pinching today, in our wasteful consumer economy, and that's what it was – penny-pinching. But then it was necessary and it taught me that a penny saved can be more important than a penny earned, because there was very little money to be earned. Sometimes in business the revenue stream can dry up, the cashflow goes negative and you gotta keep your head above water.

My darkest hour was in 1987 when we bought the Renault Ireland distribution company for a dollar weighted down by $20 million of debt, and losing $3 million a year. For the first twelve months we worked 24/7, reducing headcount, cutting costs and selling off assets. At the same time we were trying to exude confidence and initiating marketing actions to lift the brand. In the middle of all that our primary bankers wanted to pull the plug – cease trading, chequebooks frozen, end of the road stuff.

Well, we went to see them and did a great job convincing them that they would lose everything if we ceased trading, and they gave us three months to get some positive results on the board. We got a few lucky breaks and the economy picked up and we eventually pulled ourselves up out of the red ink.

Renault Ireland is now a highly successful company in the motor trade premier league. But back then in the dark days of 1987 we had to hold on with our fingernails to keep the ship afloat. It's true what they say – the darkest hour is just before dawn. So have courage, be resilient, fight on and you can win through.

YOU ARE NUMBER ONE

Molly Darcy told me many times, 'You are number one, you are the eldest boy in this family and it's your job to take care of the younger ones. So we need you to stay strong and healthy and you have to be responsible for yourself first to be able to look after the others. You are the warrior.'

From my earliest days I was trained to think on my feet, to be proactive, to make decisions and be responsible for the consequences of those decisions. To take a wider view and consider all the players. To anticipate the result of my actions, and to act in a way that would achieve the desired result. To realise that my work today created a result tomorrow and today's world was created by my past choices. If I was unhappy today it was because of yesterday's decisions and the only person to blame when things went wrong was myself.

So we all have to realise those fundamental facts sooner or later. You have to take responsibility for the world and the life you live in today. Yes, you can moan that others were a bad influence, you can point out that you got a poor start, a neglected upbringing, little or no education. Yes, you can say you didn't get the breaks, you had bad luck. Yes, you can complain you were held back. Well guess what? It's time to put all that behind you. It's time to appreciate the many talents and abilities you do have, to start increasing your talents and improving your abilities. It's time for you to convince yourself that you can succeed, you can be a winner, you can be number one.

You become a number one by winning. Win at small things first, by setting yourself small goals, daily tasks, that you achieve and tick the box. Feel the glow of success for small things, and over time you will be achieving bigger and more meaningful objectives. You will start to believe in your ability to achieve, and as your success builds your confidence grows. Extra confidence gives you the strength to keep going when times get tough, to handle positively the occasional failures. It teaches you that failures are a learning curve to success.

You become number one by believing in yourself and in your ability to achieve and realising that the only failure is not to try to be an achiever. It's by trying that you will realise the untapped potential you have, it's by trying and failing that you grow stronger, it's by trying that you will start wining, and when you start to win you get to like winning, then you're on a roll and you become a winner – numero uno!

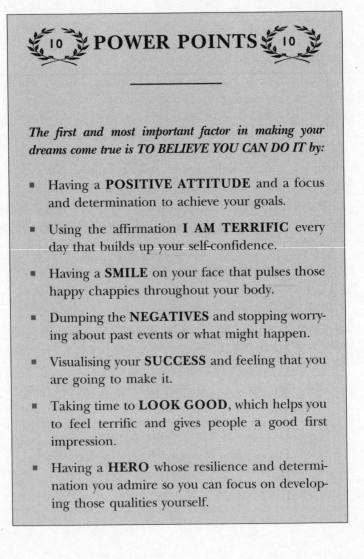

10 POWER POINTS 10

The first and most important factor in making your dreams come true is TO BELIEVE YOU CAN DO IT by:

- Having a **POSITIVE ATTITUDE** and a focus and determination to achieve your goals.

- Using the affirmation **I AM TERRIFIC** every day that builds up your self-confidence.

- Having a **SMILE** on your face that pulses those happy chappies throughout your body.

- Dumping the **NEGATIVES** and stopping worrying about past events or what might happen.

- Visualising your **SUCCESS** and feeling that you are going to make it.

- Taking time to **LOOK GOOD**, which helps you to feel terrific and gives people a good first impression.

- Having a **HERO** whose resilience and determination you admire so you can focus on developing those qualities yourself.

3

P – A DYNAMIC
PLAN OF ACTION

- As The Twig Is Bent
- Your Future Doesn't Just Happen
- Know Your Core Values
- Capture The Vision – Write It Down
- The Wheel Of Lifetime Success
- Ten Out Of Ten
- Here's An Extra Four Hours A Day
- Every Day, Without Fail, No Excuses
- Do It Now
- It's Never Too Late

AS THE TWIG IS BENT

From the time I was six years old I was an early riser. Up early to get Mass with the Ma before we went to buy her fruit in the Dublin Fruit Markets. Up early to catch the first train with Molly Darcy to meet the trawlers at dawn in Howth harbour to buy her fish. Up early to catch the bus to the farms where we harvested the fruit and vegetables in summertime.

Initially it meant going to bed early in line with the old proverb, 'Early to bed and early to rise is the way to be healthy, wealthy and wise.'

But as I got into my late teens, I could do with five or six hours' sleep easily. The habit of getting up early was ingrained in me. My alcohol-free lifestyle was a great help, and today I have my mother's habit of about four to five hours' sleep a night. When you have Action Steps* and Wow Projects*, life is an exciting challenge that you want to seize at the crack of dawn. The activities in my office start at the six o'clock mark and anyone coming in after nine gets a 'Good Afternoon' greeting.

So, the Wheel Of Lifetime Success and its Plan Of Action is something that older teenagers should adopt. It will enable them to identify their core values at an early stage of life. It will guide them in the right direction and let them focus on maximum achievement and realise their potential in a structured manner.

All teenagers have dreams and it's the responsibility of parents and teachers to help nurture those dreams. My mother encouraged and guided me every day of her life:

* See page 58 (Wow Projects), page 60 (Action Steps).

'Of course you're going to make it to the top – you are the best seller on the street.'

My grandmother nurtured my spirit for achievement:

'You have warrior's blood in your veins – you need never fear any man.'

My father was a big strong champion boxer and a former soldier:

'You are the best soccer player on the pitch – you could play for Ireland.'

Young people need encouragement, need guidance, and if they get that support at an early age they will be achievers. The determination to achieve their dreams can be strengthened, the passion for achievement will be ignited, and they will embrace the habits of success.

In 1994 a fourteen-year-old Irish lad from County Kildare who loved to ride horses took a challenge from his father: if his son didn't drink or smoke until he was twenty-one he'd get a thousand pounds. The lad had already shown natural talent in local show-jumping competitions. With focused determination, and encouraged by his parents and grandparents, he set his sights on winning an Olympic medal for Ireland in Athens in 2004. He meticulously plotted a programme to reach that goal. Then with personal dedication and exceptional commitment Cian O'Connor planned his action steps to success.

1. Find and secure a really good horse.
2. Win a national show-jumping event.
3. Secure a generous sponsor.
4. Meet the best show-jumpers and learn from them.
5. Get a terrific coach/trainer.
6. Practise, get the results, practise.

7. Make the Irish show-jumping team.
8. Win an international event.
9. Practise, practise, practise.
10. Make the Irish Olympic Squad.
11. Practise, every day, no excuses.
12. Make the Athens Olympic team.
13. Win an Olympic Medal.

On the side of his horsebox in twelve-inch-high letters, Cian printed his affirmation:

'Working Towards The Athens Olympics.'

In 2001 he collected the one thousand pound bet from his dad and continued to abstain from smoking and drinking. On Friday 27 August 2004 he won the gold medal in the twilight glow of the Athens Olympics. At twenty-four years old he was the youngest rider ever to win the gold. He had the warrior's attitude for achievement and he created his own success.

Cian O'Connor and
Waterford Crystal Gold Medal Winners 2004 Olympics

'As The Twig Is Bent,
So Shall The Tree Grow'

After this book went to the printer the controversy over positive or negative testing results on Cian's horse emerged. His gold medal win was tarnished. But you know what, I'll bet a pound to a penny that Cian O'Connor will win an Olympic medal in the Beijing Olympics 2008. This young man is a determined, focused achiever. He is hard-working, professional, an expert in every aspect of the horse jumping business. For me Cian O'Connor is a man of great integrity and it's my belief his resilience and his strength of character will bring him worldwide success and respect.

YOUR FUTURE DOESN'T JUST HAPPEN

Where you are in life today is the result of the decisions you took in the past. Every action has a consequence, so today you are experiencing the consequences of past actions. More often it's the consequences of past inactions that have created any disappointments you feel today, because not making a decision is a decision. You had better realise that you are the person who can create your own future by taking responsibility for your actions and make sure that the decisions you take today will create the future you want.

Do you know exactly where you want to go with your life? Where you intend to be in ten or twenty or thirty years' time? Will you still be in the job you are in now? Would you prefer to be in the boss's job? So very few people ask themselves the question and even fewer answer it, and fewer still do anything about it even if they have an answer.

The first thing you need to do to reach your goal is to know exactly what success means to you. Success doesn't necessarily mean you want bundles of money, or lots of possessions. It certainly does mean you want to enjoy good health. But you need to think about what you would like your destination to be and how you'd like to travel there. Remember that where you are now is where your previous planning has taken you.

Have you big dreams? Like to walk on the moon one day? Want to own a McDonald's fast food franchise? Want to be a Senator? Or an airline pilot? Want to be the richest man on the planet or win a gold medal at the Olympics? Are these just wishful thinking, mere daydreams, or do you really have a dream you would love to make happen? Would you really, really love to be the chief executive and owner of a major company in the business you know best?

Well, the only way that's going to happen is if you get really serious about it, and write it down on your Plan of Action. Then get yourself some extra time by dumping time wasters and make the time to focus on the Action Steps that you decide. That's how you start. It's great to dare to dream. It's even greater to do something about making it happen. You have to take responsibility for yourself because . . .

Your Future Doesn't Just Happen You Create It.

KNOW YOUR CORE VALUES

It's important to accept that it doesn't really matter where you are today and how badly adrift you are from where you want to be. You just need to focus on what really matters to you. What really matters to you is reflected in your core values and these can be identified under headings like these:

- Your Integrity
- Your Family
- Your Friends
- Your Career
- Your Finances
- Your Charities
- Your Property
- Your Happiness
- Your Community
- Your Dreams
- Your Leisure
- Your Health
- Your Education
- Your Wow Projects

You may have others but it's in these headings that most people's core values are covered. In fact it's usual that you can contain all the things that really matter to you under just ten core values:

You: Your health, personal development, integrity

Family: Your spouse, children, family, siblings

Career: Your job, business

People: Your colleagues, friends, acquaintances, network

Fun: Your leisure, holidays, sport, happiness

Finances: Your earnings, investments, savings, property

Community: Your charities, community supports

Education: Study, read books, learning

Dreams: Your big dreams for the future

Wow Projects: Your most exciting ambitions

There are other core values you can focus on. Some of them can be included under my ten headings or you can expand the ten into twelve or more if you wish. But why not focus on your ten most important ones? When you've made some considerable progress in those ten areas you can bring in others. Also, you can fit in many items under each of the ten headings. For example:

Integrity	*You*
Honesty	*You*
Spiritual	*You*
Leadership	*You*
Happiness	*Fun*
Ambitions	*You*
Generosity	*Community*
Learning	*Career or You*
Selling Skills	*Career*
Lose Weight	*Health*
Live Longer	*Health*
Fly A Helicopter	*Wow*

It's up to you now to write out your list of ten core values and to help you I am listing the ten that I presently use. Have a look and see how you could align yours with them.

1. You: Look after yourself first. You are your first priority. You are a unique, wonderful creation and it's your first responsibility to nurture yourself. Nurture your body by exercising to fitness. Eat properly to be healthy inside and out, to strengthen your immune system. Be strong to radiate vitality. You can live healthy to one hundred.

2. Family: Your spouse/partner is your next priority. To care for them and protect them as you would yourself. You should help your spouse/partner to grow with you as you develop as a person and a parent. Nurture your children who are the source of your greatest joy. Put your family before all others.

3. Career: Find the career you like and then be passionate about being the best at what you do. Give added value to your employer. Outwork your colleagues. Be available for extra tasks and grab those opportunities in which you will stand out from the crowd.

4. People: Life is all about people. Your friends, colleagues, acquaintances. Keep your people database up to date. Talk to those strangers you meet and you'll make a lot of new friends. Keep in touch. Send a handwritten note to at least one person a day.

5. Fun: Take time out for fun, for leisure, for family time, for sport, for holidays, for enjoyment. Golf and tennis are the two most popular sports on the planet. Tennis is the people friendly one which I enjoy most. Be a participator not a spectator. Mixed tennis doubles combines family, friends, fun and exercise. Make tennis a weekly event in your life.

6. Finances: Money doesn't always bring happiness but without money life can be tough. You will focus on fast tracking your career using the Six Simple Steps To Success to gain promotion. Or pack up your employment to be an entrepreneur and start your own business. But be sure you have gained the expertise to succeed while you are working for someone else. Do more than you are paid to do and you'll soon be paid a lot more for what you do!

7. Community: We all have a duty to give support to our community. The school which educates your kids, local and international charities, your community centre, your favourite charity. Help those who are less well off.

8. Education: One of the most important things in your life. Although I was expelled from school at thirteen years old, I went to night school for five years to get further education. I read six books every week at that time. I was learning, learning, learning. Education is even more important today, so it has to be one of your primary values. Never stop learning.

9. Dreams: We all have dreams. To live in a mansion, to write a book, to be a scratch golfer, to be an international soccer player. Take these special dreams and put them into your Wheel of Lifetime Success*. For twenty years I wanted to write the story of my dynamic mother. When I eventually made it happen my *Penny Apples* book became an international best-seller – *my* dream come true. Write down your dreams if you really want them to come true.

10. Wow: This is my special projects segment where I put the most exciting, fun things I want to do like Walk the Channel Tunnel (done✓); Ride in a Hot Air Balloon (done✓); Stand on the Statute of Christ in Rio de Janeiro (done✓); play golf with Darren Clarke (done✓ – next year Tiger); ride a horse in the cowboy country of Arizona (done✓); dinner with the US President in the White House (done✓); and meet Queen Elizabeth (done✓). Tom Peters named these his Wow Projects. Achieve some of your Wow Projects and you'll have a Wow of a life!

* See Pages 61, 62, 63

CAPTURE THE VISION – WRITE IT DOWN

In this high-tech world we live in we have adjusted to the new ways of communication and learning. Computers, email, mobile phones, distant learning, text messaging, voicemail, faxing. All of these, and more to come, are taking communications forward in huge leaps.

But when it comes to your Plan of Action you must write it down. Why? Because your brain and your pen are connected, big time! When you write down, 'I will be a millionaire in five years from today', your brain wakes up, it concentrates, this is personal. So that thought is not just written on paper, it's in the front of your brain, written in stone, because you see it in your planner every day.

Yes, we use affirmations to support our goals and we say, 'I am terrific' every morning before we leave the house. But you write down 'I Will Be A Millionaire In Five Years From Today' and that becomes a belief, a challenge. Your brain will push you to do something about it.

The thought processes of your brain push those words into the Very Important Category much more strongly than if you said it, or dictated it, or typed it. Writing with your pen is a combination of your physical, mental and spiritual senses that leaves an indelible mark on your psyche. It is absorbed into your subconscious every time you read it. Your handwritten words often flow from your pen without thinking. Your goal becomes part of your inner self which will dictate the actions you need to take to achieve that goal.

So start by allocating a tabbed section of your planner to each individual core value. Planners or organisers come in many formats – Franklin Covey, Day Timer, FiloFax, Day

Runner, or indeed our own Golden Apples version – and they all have a tabbed section for core values.

In each tabbed section you allocate a page for every goal you can think of under that core value heading. It's on that page that you then write the script of your steps to achieve that goal. Prioritise those steps, give a time frame to each step right up to the achievement of the goal.

1. Write down your core values.

2. Write down the focus points of your core values.

3. Prioritise three focus points and complete your wheel.

4. Make out a goal sheet for each focus point.

5. Write down the action steps to achieve the goal with a time frame.

6. Start moving the action steps to your To Do list.

Visualise the achievement, go and make it happen.
Sounds simple? That's because it is simple.

THE WHEEL OF LIFETIME SUCCESS

Man's greatest invention was the wheel, the cog on which not just transportation but machines of all descriptions were invented. The wheel has moved mountains and was the very foundation of modern civilisation.

The WHEEL of LIFETIME SUCCESS

SUGGESTED CORE VALUES

WHEN YOU HAVE A CONFIDENT CAN-DO ATTITUDE
FOR ACHIEVING, AND COMMIT TO USING YOUR TIME
EFFECTIVELY, YOU ARE ON A SPRINGBOARD TO SUCCESS.
YOUR ENERGY WILL CASCADE INTO
ALL THE SEGMENTS OF YOUR CORE VALUES.

The WHEEL of LIFETIME SUCCESS

SUGGESTED FOCUS POINTS

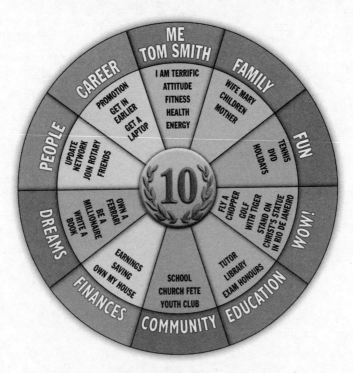

WHEN YOU HAVE A CONFIDENT CAN-DO ATTITUDE
FOR ACHIEVING, AND COMMIT TO USING YOUR TIME
EFFECTIVELY, YOU ARE ON A SPRINGBOARD TO SUCCESS.
YOUR ENERGY WILL CASCADE INTO
ALL THE SEGMENTS OF YOUR FOCUS POINTS.

The WHEEL of LIFETIME SUCCESS

MAKE YOUR OWN WHEEL

WHEN YOU HAVE A CONFIDENT CAN-DO ATTITUDE
FOR ACHIEVING, AND COMMIT TO USING YOUR TIME
EFFECTIVELY, YOU ARE ON A SPRINGBOARD TO SUCCESS.
YOUR ENERGY WILL CASCADE INTO
ALL THE SEGMENTS OF YOUR CORE VALUES.

So I use the wheel to symbolise my Plan of Action, to keep the overview in front of me all the time. The Wheel of Lifetime Success lets you see the three focus points of your ten core values at a glance on one single page.

On Page 61 you have the wheel with a suggested ten core values. Page 62 you have the wheel with my three focus points for each value. On Page 63 you have a blank wheel which you can photocopy and fill in your own choices in both values and priorities. As you progress in achieving your goals you should review and refocus your three priorities on a regular basis.

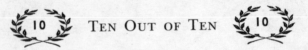

TEN OUT OF TEN

Ten is the magic figure, the peak of achievement. In school our teacher said it was the ultimate perfection. In mathematics your answer could win you the ten for complete accuracy. But in literature, in history, in languages, the ten was the teacher's subjective opinion.

In the Olympics you could win the race, jump higher and longer or break the world record to be the winner and claim the ten. But in gymnastics, in figure skating, it was the judges' subjective opinion. The ten is also an ever rising bar. Your brilliant performance today achieves ten but next month that performance is outclassed and you have to be better than before to claim the ten. This is the journey of continuous improvement.

Muhammad Ali went to the Rome Olympics in 1960 as the young eighteen-year-old Golden Gloves Champion, Cassius Clay. He made his own special journey to the Coliseum, where he stood on the Emperor's Balcony, where

Muhammad Ali and Sonny Liston

Nero had given the thumbs up or down to declare the death or spare the life of a gladiator.

The young boxer was in his own zone as he visualised the packed stadium roaring 'Hail Cassius! Hail to our hero.' His full name was Cassius Marcellus Clay, after a Roman General. He was convinced he was destined for greatness, which would commence in this Roman city by winning Olympic gold. What a surge of endorphins he must have felt, believing he would triumph in his spiritual home. A destiny he was born for.

That evening, when Cassius returned to the Olympic village he watched the gymnasts at practice: high rings, parallel bars, vaulting horse, floor acrobatics. The question of who wins. The old Chinese instructor told him about the ten out of ten. No knockout wins in gymnastics, it's the subjective opinion of the judges.

'And you, young man, in the boxing arena face the same challenge. Not to maim your opponent but to show your boxing skills, your physical strength and your mental resilience. Your speed of hand and foot. Your co-ordination of mind and body. The lightning reflexes of a superior athlete. In this way you become the best and attain ten out of ten. Success is a journey not a destination.'

That week the young boxer started his journey of continuous improvement by winning Olympic Gold. He focused on being the best he could be. The rest is history.

I have always used the Greek winners' laurel wreath with the number ten in its centre as my personal symbol of continuous improvement. Your lifetime success is about using your time effectively to gain the achievements you have targeted for success in your life. The ten is your motivation to pursue the habits of success.

HERE'S AN EXTRA FOUR HOURS A DAY

Time is the secret of your lifetime success. Do you spend it wisely or do you waste it frivolously? We all get twenty-four hours every day and how you use those hours will dictate the achievements of your life. Use your time and energy on the things that have value for you and your life will be enhanced and you will rapidly achieve your goals.

So do an audit of how you use your precious time. You'll see for yourself just how much of your time slips away wastefully. The biggest timewaster is TV; we all sit in front of this box looking at inane productions. There are more

66

hours spent watching TV than working. Think about it, all the kids watching, the unemployed watching, the workforce after work watching. TV is now the number one national inactivity. Make a big difference in your lifestyle by limiting your TV time to a maximum of one hour a day. Enjoy the comedy shows, some sport maybe, and get the news on the radio in your car. But as from today, cut your TV viewing in half.

Travel time, to and from work, has become a nightmare for all of us. The solution for me was flexitime. I leave home by 5.30 in the morning and head back home at 4 p.m. If I miss the early morning slot, I don't leave until 10 a.m. So my eighteen mile journey takes no more than thirty minutes. If I left between 7 a.m. and 8 a.m. the trip would take one and a half hours. So for me it's all about timing and using that flexitime. One day a week I work from home, which can be even more productive and adds on some extra quality time too.

If you do spend a lot of time in the car or in the train be sure to use the power of CDs for music relaxation, or for learning from the excellent motivational products from Anthony Robbins, Tom Peters, Deepak Chopra or other wise teachers. On page 70 you have a Time Audit that lets you focus on your own time priorities. You can find at least an extra twenty hours a week for yourself. A priceless gift if you know what to do with it.

In this new millennium we have zillions of time-saving gadgets. Fast boiling teapots, microwave ovens, motor cars, washing machines, iPods, computers, PDAs, escalators, mobile phones, the list is endless. Yet we live in a time poor society. We have no time for the kids, no time to visit friends, no time to go to the gym, no time for ourselves.

The way to give yourself more time is to **take control of your time**. That's why you should do the time audit (page 70) and have a good look at how you use your time.

Reorganise and prioritise your time and you will take control of your time. Be serious about your priorities, what is really important for you to do. It's not about doing more and more, it's not about going fast, it's about being in control so you can take it easy.

When I drive up the motorway to the office at 5.30 in the morning I have a clear run. Very few cars on the road. For some magic reason all the traffic lights are green. I'm relaxed listening to Maxi play her soothing music on the radio. Feeling fresh and engerised after my *Golden Apples* fitness exercises. Flicking over in my mind the priority items I'm to focus on. The no-hassle way to start the day.

If for some reason I can't leave the house before 6.15 a.m., I just stay at home and work from the den – ring the office where my assistant can fax any items that need attention.

Write some handwritten notes, review some current projects and clear the paperwork. I avoid the 6.30 a.m. to 9.30 a.m. traffic gridlocks and head off up the road in the post rush-hour lull. I won't do the two-hour car crawls. I want to stay in control of my time and still get the job done. You have to look at your own schedule and figure out what will work for you. It may take some negotiating with employers or clients to achieve a win-win situation for everyone. A bit of give and take.

Early to bed and early to rise is a good way to start. Avoid the hassles as best you can, take control of your time and you will make more time for yourself.

And as I've said before, you can reduce your sleeping

time. Try it yourself by putting your alarm clock back by two minutes a week. You won't even notice two minutes but you'll soon save yourself an hour a day in a very short seven months. And the key to less sleep is exercise. If you make sure you do your fitness plan every day (see Chapter 6) you will fall asleep quickly, and get enough deep relaxing sleep in a shorter time span that will still energise your day. Remember what Molly said – 'Sleeping is the nearest thing to dying you'll ever do, so don't do too much of it.'

WE ALL GET 24 HOURS EVERY DAY
HOW YOU USE YOUR TIME
WILL DICTATE
YOUR ACHIEVEMENTS IN LIFE

Weekday Routine	Average Guy		YOU		My Day	Saving On Average Guy Today
	Today	Possible	Today	Objective		
Sleep	8 hrs	6 hrs			5 hrs	–3 hrs
Career	8 hrs	8 hrs			12 hrs	+4 hrs
Travel Time	2 hrs	2 hrs			1 hr	–1 hr
Lunch	1 hr	1 hr			0.30	–30 mins
Dinner	1.30	1.30			1 hr	–30 mins
TV/Pub	3 hrs	1.30			0.30	–2.5 hrs
Leisure/Fun	Nil	1 hr			2.30	+2.5 hrs
Kids	Weekend	1 hr			Grown Up	–
Domestic	Weekend	Weekend			Weekend	–
Exercise	Nil	0.30			0.30	+.5 hrs
Bathroom	0.30	0.30			0.30	–
Myself	Nil	0.30			0.30	+.5 hrs
Total	24 hrs	24 hrs			24 hrs	+7.5 hrs per Day

What would you do with an extra 7.5 hours every day?

EVERY DAY, WITHOUT FAIL, NO EXCUSES

The six chapters on success in this book are filled with positive actions for you to implement. Everything you want, everything you desire, can be yours. But you have to adopt those action steps as part of your new lifestyle. Ingrain the Focus Points into your psyche as habits of success. A habit is something you do automatically, without thinking, because you have done it daily for a long time – like picking up the toothbrush when you walk into the bathroom.

So start ingraining the success habits now, today, by completing your Wheel of Lifetime Success. By listing your top three priorities as Focus Points in each segment. By writing your Goals Sheets and moving some Action Steps on to your To Do list.

On your daily To Do list for the next month have four Must Do Priorities such as Fitness Plan, Vitamins, Power Juice and Early Start as the key activities you want to ingrain as success habits. And for the next month make sure you do them every day, without fail, no excuses. Keep them on your To Do list until they are daily habits that you do without thinking.

Then, month by month, move in other items that you want to become habits like:

Up at 5 a.m.

Write A Note

Tell Mary I Love Her

Take The Dog For A Walk

and work on those four until they become ingrained habits.

Guess what happens when you take these habits on board as daily activities? You get a double whammy, because some old timewasters have to be pushed aside. Like doing couch potato and TV junk. Like hanging out with the negative people. As the new habits become ingrained, your positive results will start to flow from a trickle to a stream. A stream of achievements that will change your life. But that will only happen – if *you* make it happen.

DO IT NOW

Every mature adult has had enough experiences in life to enable them to write a book. Millions of people have said, 'I know so much about that subject I could write a book about it.' Thousands of people really want to write a book, but they never get around to it. Why?

Many people want to lose weight. In the first week of January every year millions of people around the world join a gym. They pay millions of dollars for a year's subscription. Full of Christmas fare, full of enthusiasm, they pay up and sign on the dotted line. After just two weeks, by 15 January, having used less than five per cent of the value of the year's subscription, more than sixty per cent of those enthusiasts throw in the towel. By 1 February more than seventy-five per cent of them have fallen off the wagon. That's right – they pack it in – never to go back again. Why?

In the same first week of January every year millions of people make their New Year's resolutions. To eat less, to exercise more, to lose weight, to get promoted, to learn a language, to take an educational course, to visit mother more often. This list is endless and its demise is the same. Gone and forgotten after a few weeks. Why?

The answer they give is that they don't have time. No time for writing or exercising or learning. But what is time? It's not the twenty-four hours a day we have – it's what we do with those twenty-four hours. That's what time really is. How we use the hours!

We all remember past events but we don't remember the days we did nothing.

Think about that for a minute. Some people can lie on a couch for five hours, reading newspapers, and eating a burger while watching TV. Is that time? No. It's time wasting! Other people, in the same five hours, fit in two hours on the tennis court, two hours on a computer skills course, and an hour at a charity fund-raising meeting. Now *that's* time well spent. And it's the time well spent that brings achievements and the time wasted is lost for ever.

In essence you have to use time well for time to be real for you. Sleep time and leisure activities are time well spent, but not the other lazy, do nothing, boring time wasting non-activities that so many of us indulge in so often.

The solution to time wasting is to have a Plan of Action where you have Action Steps from all your Goal Sheets listed on your To Do list. Your Plan Of Action should always include specific fun, leisure and pleasure activities that you will enjoy.

Aways have activities lined up that are productive, that will take you further on the journey to achieving your goals.

Keep your Action Steps at the ready, choose one of the priorities and **do it now**. That way you'll have buckets of time, and every evening you'll enjoy the warm glow of achievement.

'Yesterday is history, tomorrow is a mystery, you only have today – use it well.' – Molly Darcy.

IT'S NEVER TOO LATE

Molly Darcy lived for one hundred years (1892–1992). She was hale and hearty all her life and she didn't get any of our modern diseases. In her later years she was always lucid and participated in family conversations. We'd joke with her about having her passport through the Pearly Gates and she'd say, 'You know son, we all want to go to Heaven, but not yet.'

I believe the secret of longevity is keeping busy and thinking young. I add two or three Goal Sheets a week to my schedule and try to clear a similar number. So I keep busy with positive, exciting Action Steps and get a great sense of achievement as I complete purposeful projects.

As for thinking young, my fitness plan has helped me have robust good health and I have the energy of a youngster. I visit thirty schools a year and many of our charity youth projects. Remember what I said to that broker amazed to see my planned retirement date at 2050? 'When I'm hundred and eight, I hope to get another twenty-two years to really have some fun.'

The point is that I believe we all have the physical potential to live healthily to one hundred. We have learned more about health and nutrition, and realise that it's our own abuse that reduces our life spans.

The life expectancies for men and women are stretching longer and longer. In the 1950s anyone over fifty years of age was considered old. The fact that those generations had endured two world wars and the accompanying economic deprivations influenced that perception. But today a fifty year old is enjoying the prime of life and we see seventy-year-olds who are fresh as a daisy!

No matter what age you are you can use my *Golden Apples* to make the rest of your life the very best of your life. Identify your core values, get the Wheel Of Lifetime Success into gear, and get yourself moving in a busy new lifestyle. Go out and meet people and make new friends.

If you are a young person, focus on learning. Get your exams. When you move into a job be the best at it and stand out from the crowd. Help people and they will help you. Work harder and better and create the opportunities to move upwards and onwards. Use your Wheel to achieve your goals. Sure, you go and enjoy yourself at weekends, but put the effort into securing your future during the week.

No matter what age you are or where you are in your chosen career, use the Wheel to help you focus on what you want to do, where you want to go and how you are going to get there. You have the ability and the talent to achieve your goals. Your plan of action is the key to making it all happen for you.

If you are retired, get involved with the grandchildren. Take three shots off your golf handicap. Learn a new language in a school with other students. Realise that every day you can get out of bed is a great day. It's about getting busy and enjoying your life.

I've convinced myself that I'll achieve ten times more in the next forty years than I have in the past sixty-three. Optimistic is what you can call that, but that's my attitude for achievement shining through.

> 'Make The Rest Of Your Life
> The Best Of Your Life'

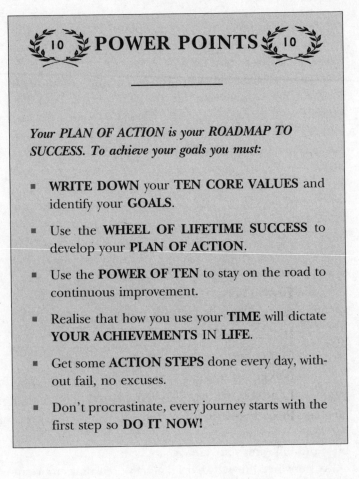

POWER POINTS

Your PLAN OF ACTION is your ROADMAP TO SUCCESS. To achieve your goals you must:

- **WRITE DOWN** your **TEN CORE VALUES** and identify your **GOALS**.

- Use the **WHEEL OF LIFETIME SUCCESS** to develop your **PLAN OF ACTION**.

- Use the **POWER OF TEN** to stay on the road to continuous improvement.

- Realise that how you use your **TIME** will dictate **YOUR ACHIEVEMENTS** IN **LIFE**.

- Get some **ACTION STEPS** done every day, without fail, no excuses.

- Don't procrastinate, every journey starts with the first step so **DO IT NOW!**

4
P – PEOPLE POWER

- Smile – It's Good For You
- How To Be A Great Conversationalist
- Always Speak In The Positive
- It's All About People
- Make People Feel Special
- Never Squeeze A Friendship
- Leaders Are Made – Not Born
- Power Points

SMILE – IT'S GOOD FOR YOU

I would have never reached the height of my achievements without the help and support I received from so many people. Of course you can expect help from parents, from family, from friends. But the more help you get the better for you, so be sure to make a lot of friends as soon as you can. Because life and business is all about people – people who can give a hand, open doors, get you introductions, give you the business.

The Irish are famous for their gift of the blarney and their hospitality. We love to talk, to meet people, to help people, and will always be quick to make contact with strangers – in a bar, on the plane. We are first to smile, to nod, to say 'Hello, how are you?' We're good communicators.

On the road to high achievement, people skills are a priority. It's a subject you don't see on college curricula and it's the platform for success in any profession or business. You will always need help along the way and if people like you they will want to help you. So the secret of getting help from people is to get people to like you, which means making a positive impact on them and – more importantly – making them feel good.

The first way to make a positive impact on people is to smile. Molly Darcy gave me that advice when I was a child:

'I met a man today who didn't have a smile so I gave him one – and he gave me one back.'

People will always react positively to a smile and it gives a clear signal that you are easygoing, sociable and friendly.

Smiling is infectious
You catch it like the flu
When someone smiled at me today
I started smiling too
I passed around the corner
And someone saw my grin
When he smiled, I realized
I'd passed it on to him.
I thought about that smile,
Then realized its worth,
A single SMILE just like mine
Could travel round the earth.
So if you feel a smile begin,
Don't leave it undetected.
Let's start an epidemic quick
And get the world infected!

You can't smile at someone without also looking them in the eye. As well as making a positive connection with someone, a smile makes you feel good. The muscular action releases those endorphins into your system, the happy chappies that give you a tingling feeling of zest and goodwill. People want to be with someone who makes them feel good so your smiling face prompts them to smile back and bingo! You have given them the happy chappies that makes them feel good too. Make eye contact, smile and say, 'Hi, I'm Bill', with your hand out. The response will always be, 'Hello, my name is Brian', and you'll get a shakehands. Contact – friendly, positive communication that opens the way for rapport. Smile and the world smiles with you, cry and you'll cry alone.

HOW TO BE A GREAT CONVERSATIONALIST

The most important thing to do now is to lodge Brian's name in your head, and you do that by getting him talking. So ask a question.

'Where are you from, Brian?' Visualise him in the garments of our great warrior, Brian Boru, fighting the Vikings. Before he finishes his answer you have him lodged in your mental computer and you use his name in every sentence with him as you go along.

'Hey, so you're a Kerryman are you? You know, Brian, I spend a lot of time in Kerry; do you know Senator Paul Coghlan, my good friend in Killarney?'

The picture in your head and the use of the name will give you instant recall in the future.

Then remember Molly Darcy's other advice: 'You've got

two ears, and one mouth for a very good reason.' Listen more than you talk. Ask questions and let Brian do the talking and use open questions that can't have a 'yes' or 'no' answer.

You should listen carefully to what Brian is saying. Not just to hear the words but to realise the meaning and feelings behind the words. Don't interrupt except with a nod of the head or an understanding exclamation like 'I know what you mean'. Never anticipate what Brian is going to say by finishing a sentence for him. Bite your tongue. Don't try to match his story with a better one. Don't be thinking of what you're going to say next when you should be listening to him.

You will be amazed at how good a conversationalist Brian will think you are when you say very little and keep asking open questions that let him talk away. Then you'll soon have an exchange of business cards and a new addition to your networking contacts. A friend in the making. Just remember, when it comes to being a great conversationalist, you don't get intoxicated by the exuberance of your own verbosity. It's far better to say nothing until you hear more.

ALWAYS SPEAK IN THE POSITIVE

There's one phrase I would sincerely ask you not to use. A phrase you could hear a hundred times over if you were doing the rounds of a shopping mall. A phrase that the user intends as friendly communication but always comes across as negative. It goes like this.

You make a purchase in a store, collect your goods and receipt and you say 'Thanks very much' to the shop assistant. The response, 'No problem', always leaves me cold.

Why do people think that saying 'No problem' will make me feel good? Problem is a negative word. It conjures up anxiety, and certainly doesn't make me feel good at all. And the word 'no' is one of the least liked words in the dictionary. It takes you back to the disappointed times you experienced – **NO** you can't have an ice cream, **NO** you can't go out to play with Tommy, **NO** you can't have a new bicycle.

So why give a guest, a customer, a friend these two negative words in an attempt to make them feel good? We haven't thought it through because it originated in a cartoon series. Bart Simpson's way of being nice became a fad!

Why not use a positive word instead? Like this:

'Thanks very much for your help.' Use the response, 'It's a pleasure.' Isn't that a lovely word? Makes me feel good to hear. Makes you feel good to say it.

The word 'pleasure' rolls off the lips in a way that makes you smile. It then provokes warm feelings in the recipient, who will return the smile. It's a reminder of warm pleasant memories – 'Of course you can have an ice cream', and 'Yes, off you go and play with Tommy' and 'Hey, look at the new bicycle I got you.' So if you really want to generate warm feelings drop the negatives and give people pleasure instead. Get into the habit of responding with 'It's a pleasure' and see how well you'll feel using it every day. You'll also see the warm smile it generates from the people you give it to.

IT'S ALL ABOUT PEOPLE

You can use the number ten to measure achievement in all the arenas of life. In your personal relationships would you give yourself a ten as a wife, as a husband, as a partner, as a parent? Do you really take time every day to build your important relationships, to care, to be aware, to even just be there? To make a phone call, to write a little note. To remember the birthdays, and that it's the thought not the gift that counts.

In business the ten has been my guiding light. I mark myself out of ten every day on my way home in the car. Did I make a ten today, get the priorities done, focus on the positives, coach the team, handle the difficult things well, did I make progress? In the same way I evaluate the contribution of our executive team who all have a number to reflect their varied contributions – and on which their yearly performance bonus is based.

I also use the ten to help us focus on our most important business asset – people. Do we get a ten for customer care, for how we treat the people who do business with us, the customers who pay our salaries? Do we put ourselves in the customers' shoes, take care of the problem the way we would like it taken care of ourselves? Do we try to give every customer a hassle-free experience? Even when tempers rise can we keep our cool and remember to be nice? The purpose of every business is to develop customers for life.

If you want your staff to take care of your customers you need to keep your staff happy and positive too. That's why we have staff parties every few months to celebrate our achievements. It may just be a little drinks and canapés session in the pub. It may be a mystery one-day train trip. It's definitely a big Christmas party and on special achievement occasions it's a weekend in a European capital city like Paris, Prague, Barcelona, Dubrovnik. For exceptional individual performances there are sunshine holidays in a luxury villa in Portugal. We also have our Renault Training Institute, where we develop the skills of our people starting with induction courses as soon as they join the company.

We also support specialist training with subsidies for college fees and tuition. Your staff, your people, your colleagues will make or break your business. Recruit the best, train them well, reward their achievements, and make sure they are passionate about achieving the company objectives by taking care of their customers. Your staff are your number one asset – always attach the list to your balance sheet and evaluate their contribution.

We have a third group of people that we want to take care of as well. Yes, we try to look after our staff so in turn they will try to look after our customers. But I also believe we have a duty to help the communities where we make our profits. At Renault, we focus on children, particularly in the disadvantaged communities and we contribute more than five per cent of our annual profits to charities. With the Irish Youth Foundation we foster and help youth projects all over Ireland through sports clubs, community centres, support groups and schools. We want every young person to get the opportunity to achieve their potential.

I visit two schools a month to help motivate the youngsters. Landing the chopper in the schoolyard, giving a one hour seminar on what they should focus on and how to be successful, taking a Q & A session and giving four lucky youngsters a trip around their town in the chopper. Hopefully leaving behind some inspirational thoughts that will lead to positive actions from the teachers and the youngsters. Waking up a passion to excel, to be the best they can be.

So it's all about people! You take care of your staff and they in turn will take care of your customers and support you in building customers for life. You help the less well-off and in caring for the community you will enhance your business. What goes around comes around!

MAKE PEOPLE FEEL SPECIAL

All my career I have used Molly Darcy's mantra of Do Unto Others. Yes, it has religious connotations as the full quotation from Matthew 7:12 is 'Do unto others as you would have them do unto you.' That is a dictum we have absorbed into our business philosophy. I have always said that the purpose of our business is to win customers for life, and the focus of every dealership is to give the customer a happy hassle-free experience. So we keep asking ourselves the questions – how would I feel about this dealer? Would I be happy with the way I was treated? We are always analysing, questioning and trying to improve, trying to do it better. Trying to make our customers feel special.

One of my ways of doing that is to send handwritten notes to people. I have always liked to write with a pen and the Christian Brothers certainly insisted on good penmanship. My Da had a lovely handwriting style and would sit down with me and show me how to use the calligraphy pens. He was always proud of his signature *William P. Cullen*. So over the years I got into the habit of answering business letters with a handwritten note. Just a one pager. When you're replying to a two page document with a one page note, you learn how to put your thoughts together in your head before you write. When you pick up the pen the ink just flows and people are always pleased to receive a handwritten note. In this age of impersonal emails a nice handwritten note will make people feel special. That's how my brain and my pen are linked together and why I found writing books a very satisfying experience.

There are lots of other ways to give people a happy experience. Corporate entertainment at big football games, and golf events. VIP tickets for the music concerts and celebrity events. But I know that the way to make people feel really special is to be nice to them in a one-on-one way. Like the handwritten note that says I took time out and gave this my personal attention. Like phoning up the customer who sends a long letter of complaint. Don't hide behind a PR response. Pick up the phone and say:

'Hi, I'm disappointed you had to write to me with this problem and I really want to make you happy – how do you think I can do that?' That's it, and you know, most people are reasonable, and we usually come to a win-win solution. As I start in the office at 6 a.m. I sometimes make these calls at 6.30 a.m. and that really gets attention.

'Jeepers I didn't realise you'd ring me about this yourself Mister Cullen. Thanks very much for your help.'

But you must make sure you follow up and that the problem really is solved.

I always carry little gifts. Something unusual. My favourite is the folding eye glasses which we have in a nice tortoise-shell case. Whenever I'm with someone who starts fumbling for their spectacles to read something I say, 'Here, try these' and hand them the case. It's a real surprise opening it up, and adjusting the reading glasses.

'Wow, they are terrific. I can see clear as day and they are so handy.'

When I say, 'You can keep them with our compliments', I always get a genuine warm smile of thanks. I was walking into a theatre one night when I got a big hello from a customer I hadn't seen for a long time. Across the foyer she waved the tortoiseshell case at me, blew me a kiss, and shouted, 'I still have them, they are terrific.'

When you absorb the **Plan of Action** in the previous chapter you should write down in your planner for every day: How Can I Make Someone Feel Special Today?

NEVER SQUEEZE A FRIENDSHIP

We sold Christmas decorations on the streets of Dublin in the month of December. Now that was a business lesson that Donald Trump should try. We stood shoulder to shoulder with a couple of hundred competitors lining the footpath in Henry Street, in the usual bleak December weather with no escape from the rain. No matter how much clothing you had on or umbrellas to get under, the rain trickled down around your neck. Seeped from head to toe it did, and there was no escape. Days when you started at seven o'clock on a twelve-hour shift. The Donald's Apprentices wouldn't last an hour!

All of us were selling the same products with the same spiel 'Get your bells, balls, balloons and tinsel. Get the dolls for the girls or the monkey on the stick to keep the ould fella from dozing.'

This is where we developed the added value concept, such as dressing the dolls like the popular celebrities of the time. 'Get your Judy Garland or your Marilyn Monroe', brought the punters flocking up to you. We had to keep

Selling balloons, 1952

looking for a competitive advantage and one of those was pricing. Could we buy at a better price?

Well, let me take another story from my *Penny Apples* book that gave me a memorable lesson in negotiation. A lesson in purchasing that some of the giant car companies should learn as they squeeze their suppliers to the bone. In this story I'm called Liam again.

'You're selling loads of balloons,' Hector Grey said to Liam one day. 'I hope you're making a good profit.' The ten-year-old youngster looked up at him.

'What's profit, Mister Grey?' he asked.

'Profit, my son,' said Hector, 'is the difference between the price you buy the balloons for and the price you sell them for.'

'Yes, Mister Grey, I think we're doing all right there with the profit,' Liam replied quickly.

Hector raised his bushy eyebrows and said, 'Well you have to do better than all right, Liam, you have to make sure you get your one per cent. You buy these balloons for sixpence a dozen. Ha'penny each. So you must sell them for a penny each. Get your one per cent profit, d'ya see what I mean?'

'Yes, I do, Mister Grey,' said Liam. 'Double your buying price is the price to sell for. Buy for a penny, sell for twopence, buy for a shilling, sell for two bob. That's the one per cent profit, is it?'

'Yes, me son, that's it,' said Hector. 'That's what ya need to make it worth your while with all the work you do. As for me, here in this shop with overheads to pay . . .' and he paused at the young lad's quizzical look. 'Overheads, Liam, is me expenses: the rent on the shop, the rates to the Corporation, the electricity bills, the shipping costs on the goods, the import taxes, the staff I employ, that's me overheads,' he explained as the young fella nodded.

'With my overheads to pay,' Hector continued, 'sure I have to get two per cent if I want to clear a few pounds at all.'

So Liam continued the balloon-selling and never forgot the wise teaching of Hector Grey, and even managed to get his own two per cent on some sales items over the years.

It was with Hector too that Liam learned about negotiating, and credit terms and bulk discounts. The first year buying from Hector, Liam saw Mother Darcy paying for her purchase on the spot. Cash up front. But the following December, after some experience with the Ma in the market, Liam watched Molly buying the stock.

Molly Darcy

'That's four pounds, seventeen shillings,' Hector said, 'but we'll round it off at four pounds fifteen shillings to you, Molly.' It was the first Saturday morning and Liam was with Mother Darcy all day because school was closed.

'Are we not good customers now, Hector?' Liam asked. 'With a track record? We must be your best buyer for balloons and we've Aunt Julie with us this year. With three of us selling on the street, we'll be your biggest customers.'

Hector looked at him. 'And that you are, Liam,' he said. 'That's why I just knocked two shillings off the price for Molly.'

Liam smiled and said, 'That's great, Hector, and thank

you very much. But at the fruit markets the Ma gets an extra bit off when she buys all her apples from the same supplier for a month. Suppose we didn't buy off Northlight and gave you all our business this year, would we get a better price?'

Hector smiled and looked at Molly. 'Now isn't this fella learning fast, Molly me girl,' he said. 'You can be sure I'll make it worth your while to buy exclusively from Hector Grey. If you buy a hundred pounds' worth off me this month, I'll refund you eight pounds. No few bob here and there. We'll add up everything you buy, and if ya go over the ton I'll give you back eight quid, and we'll run a credit line, so you don't have to pay me until Christmas. How's that?'

Before Liam could respond, Molly said, 'Well, the blessings of God on ya, Hector Grey, but aren't you the dacent man. Sure that's terrific, isn't it, Liam, and I'll shake hands on the deal.' And they did indeed shake hands.

Outside the shop, Molly said, 'Well done, Liam, that's a great deal ya got. Only now we'll really have to get working, to sell a hundred pounds' worth of stuff before Christmas.'

'We might have got a bit more off him, Molly,' Liam said.

Mother Darcy stopped her pram and looked at him. 'Son, you did a great job in there with Hector,' she said, and she smiled at him. 'And if we get the eight pounds, half of it is yours. But I also want you to remember that I've been a customer of Hector Grey for a long, long time. It's friends we are and he's helped meself and your Mammy when we needed it. So you don't squeeze a friendship. You take the price a friend gives you, so that's why I took his eight pounds when you could have squeezed him to ten. Maybe. For us, you see, a friendship is more valuable than a little money. So yes, always push for a good deal, but never push for more from a friend. You support your friends.

Business is a two-way street between the buyer and the seller. We need each other and there's more to life than money. Didn't you enjoy the man's jokes and the cup of tea he gave us and the help he's given you?'

Liam looked at his granny and nodded. She was smiling gently at him. Even her eyes were smiling. And he smiled back at her, this small woman with her hair tied up in a bun and her black shawl wrapped around her, over her white coverall. Smiled at each other privately, they did, as the swarms of Saturday-morning people rushed up and down past them. Molly put her hand out and tossed Liam's hair.

'Come on now, son, let's get up to Aunt Julie and get to work. We've a busy month ahead if we're to make that bonus of Hector's.' She grabbed the handle of the pram and away with her up the street. Liam looked after her for a long minute. He was learning to buy, he was learning to sell, and he was now learning about people and friendship. And Molly Darcy had the wisdom of the ages.

So, another great business philosophy from Molly Darcy. Business is a two-way street. Wholesalers need someone to buy their goods, and retailers need a steady supply, while both have to make some profit from the transaction. There has to be something in the deal for both parties. Molly was wise enough to know that business is about people and she reminded me of the tough times when Hector Grey had helped her out. Since then I have learned to stick with the old reliables. When you build a strong business relationship it will stay strong to keep both sides together when things go wrong.

And things do go wrong in business. I know I could do a banking deal with one of the newcomer banks and get a one per cent better deal. But I remember when my present bankers helped me over a tough spot. I might hit a tough spot again and it's that relationship that stays strong when the newcomer might run for cover. What goes around comes around so make sure you stay close to your strategic partners and never squeeze a friendship.

LEADERS ARE MADE – NOT BORN

The best people power skill you can develop is the ability to get people to do what you want them to do. The simple way to do that is to get them to *want* to do what you want them to do. That skill evolves from them respecting your integrity, trusting your vision, believing in your ability to make it happen, having faith in your warrior strength if things go wrong, and knowing you will give the utmost personal support to get the job done.

Those beliefs are only given to true leaders, whose skills have been tested in many situations, whose track record speaks for itself. So those skills are the ones you must learn in the daily routine of experience.

Show integrity in matters big or small. Let people see that your enthusiastic passion for a project is what makes things happen. Show that you've read and studied and learned to be an expert at what you do which is what produces the right future vision they can trust. Develop the strength of mind and body that has taken you through a few tough spots. Let them see that you are always ready to roll up your sleeves and work shoulder to shoulder when necessary.

Develop these abilities and your people will be with you all the way.

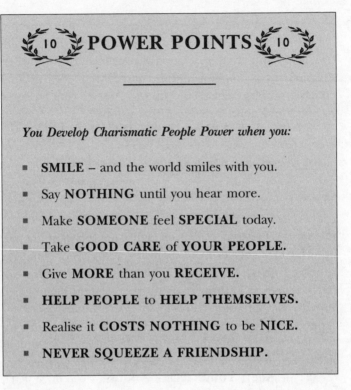

POWER POINTS

You Develop Charismatic People Power when you:

- **SMILE** – and the world smiles with you.

- Say **NOTHING** until you hear more.

- Make **SOMEONE** feel **SPECIAL** today.

- Take **GOOD CARE** of **YOUR PEOPLE.**

- Give **MORE** than you **RECEIVE.**

- **HELP PEOPLE** to **HELP THEMSELVES.**

- Realise it **COSTS NOTHING** to be **NICE.**

- **NEVER SQUEEZE A FRIENDSHIP.**

5
L – LEARN TO BE LUCKY

- Born Lucky
- Confidence Is The Key
- Learn To Be Lucky
- What Goes Around Comes Around
- It's A Small World We Live In
- Keep Your Commitments
- Create The Opportunities
- Bricks Can Be Lucky
- Make Yourself Available
- Do It Better
- Power Points

BORN LUCKY

I was born in a caul, which is the envelope a foetus lives in during gestation, and enables the baby to breathe. At birth, the caul usually bursts as the waters break and when the baby slips out into the world the remnants of the caul is part of the afterbirth.

However in about one of every 200,000 births the caul doesn't break and the doctor has to remove it from the baby. The caul is folded carefully like a sheet of tissue or parchment and the nurses always hold a little celebration of champagne with the mother on such occasions. Being born in a caul, because it's a relatively rare occurrence, is considered a very lucky omen. The preserved caul itself is much sought after by sailors and seamen who believe they can never drown if they have a caul on their person – all because the baby survived in its mother's waters during the long pregnancy.

My Uncle Bob sold my caul in 1942 at an auction in Thomas Delaney's Pub on the north docks in Dublin's port for twenty-five English pounds. The sailors during those world war years indulged in numerous superstitions, with twenty ships a day being sunk in the English Channel alone. Those twenty-five pounds were manna from heaven for my mother who used them to keep her family fed for twelve months.

As the eldest boy growing up in a large family, I had a lot of responsibility.

'Don't you know things will always work out for you, son. You are my lucky child,' the Ma would say. She called me her lucky child repeatedly and I have been blessed with good fortune all my life. Did that accident of birth create a lucky charm for me? I don't think so. The more my mother called me her lucky child the more I really believed I was lucky. I took chances as a youngster because I believed things would work out for me. And most of the time it did. I believed I would be lucky so I was lucky. I believed I could do anything. Remember Henry Ford's words:

'If You Believe You Can Or You Can't – You're Right!'

CONFIDENCE IS THE KEY

You will always hear it said of successful people that 'He was a lucky son of a gun' or, 'Sure he fell on his feet' or, 'He was in the right place at the right time'. Yes of course we all need a bit of luck but what is luck? We define it as 'opportunity meeting preparation'. We will all be given opportunities to succeed that we need to be prepared for. So the more you practise at what you want to succeed at, the readier you will be when the opportunity eventually presents itself.

But how do you make the opportunities happen? The key is confidence. The more confident you are, the more you spread yourself around, the more people who know you, then the more opportunities will arise, and the luckier you will be.

Confidence, self-esteem and self-assertiveness are not subjects that appear on school curricula. Yet they are the most precious of qualities that schools should work on developing in their students. It's often left to the parents to nurture these talents and unfortunately, for all sorts of reasons, many people are not up to the task.

I was lucky because our mother had always said, 'The best

thing I can give my children is the independence to stand on their own feet.' By sending us back to the shops to return goods in an era of gruff shopkeepers, when kids were expected to be seen and not heard, the Ma developed our self-assertiveness. 'You need a hard neck in this life.'

I can't say enough about the confidence my granny Molly Darcy developed in me, with her trick of standing me in front of a mirror to give a big smile and say 'I am terrific' twenty times. If only every kid got this counsel and used that affirmation, their confidence would grow at a rapid rate.

But Molly's use of a song from a Hollywood musical was a masterpiece. One of the hit songs from the Rodgers & Hammerstein movie *The King and I*, in which Deborah Kerr, as the English tutor to King Yul Brynner's multitude of children, decided to give the kids a lesson in confidence, 'Whenever I Feel Afraid'. The lyrics of this song are inspirational for young people and to this day I still have the words inside my organiser. It's a song and a poem to pass on to your children.

> *Whenever I feel afraid*
> *I hold my head erect*
> *And whistle a happy tune,*
> *So no one will suspect*
>   *I'm afraid.*

> *While shivering in my shoes*
> *I strike a careless pose*
> *And whistle a happy tune,*
> *And no one ever knows*
>   *I'm afraid.*

The result of this deception
Is very strange to tell,
For when I fool the people I fear
I fool myself as well!

I whistle a happy tune,
And every single time
The happiness in the tune
Convinces me that I'm,
                    Not afraid!

Make believe you're brave
And the trick will take you far;
You may be as brave
As you make believe you are.
You may be as brave
As you make believe you are.

The impact of this song reconfirms the power of the mind to fool your body into self-belief. 'Whether you believe you can or you can't – you're right.'

LEARN TO BE LUCKY

I was thirsty for knowledge after I was expelled from school. The first thing I did was to enrol in the Charliville Mall Library on the North Strand. In those days our home had an early curfew for kids: all of us had to be in bed by nine o'clock. So I got three books twice a week and read into the night with my own little torch. Over the next ten years I read every book worth reading in that library.

I also had the benefit of the *Readers' Digest*, thanks to the kind support of Mister Stack, my English teacher. He gave me a free three-year subscription when I was expelled from school, which I continued myself for many years after. In addition I bought all the condensed book special editions from the Digest Club. Anyone who has done the quiz, 'It Pays to Increase Your Word Power', in the *Readers' Digest* every month knows just how effective it is in improving your vocabulary. It is terrific.

I also enrolled in night school for three nights a week and I spent five years in the Rathmines School of Commerce, where I completed courses in Bookkeeping, Commerce, Economics, English and, guess what? Shorthand and typing. In those days typing was strictly confined to the female secretaries. But I had a free hour between classes and the only available subject for that hour was the shorthand and typing class so I signed up. I suppose the fact that I was the only guy amongst forty girls was an influencing factor. Blessed are thou amongst women.

Now let me tell you how all those hours paid off for me. One evening I was staying late in the dealership offices when the boss walked in.

'Where are the girls gone?' he asked.

'It's almost seven o'clock, Mr Wallace, they're long gone.'

'Blast it. I need this letter typed up urgently. Are you positive none of them are around?'

'Yes, I am, but you needn't worry because I can type the letter for you.'

His look of exasperation turned to one of disbelief.

'And how, may I ask, could you type a letter, and I said *type* not just write.'

'On this typewriter here, Mr Wallace. I have a typing

diploma, and you contributed twenty-five per cent of the cost of the school fees for that. So the least you can do is let me show you that you got your money's worth.'

He walked over slowly and handed me the handwritten draft. Lots of changes, and words scratched out, but I quickly put the paper in the machine and deftly typed out the letter as he looked over my shoulder. I finished with a flourish and pulled the typed letter from the carriage, which gave a professional clickety click, and handed it to him. He adjusted his reading glasses and read the letter through with a perplexed frown. He looked at me, then back at the letter, and shook his head.

'I don't believe it,' he said, 'it's perfect, absolutely perfect.'

He took out his splendid Parker fountain pen, unscrewed the gold edged cap, and carefully signed his name, then dried the ink with a sheet of blotting paper as I typed the addressee's name and address on the envelope and handed it to him.

'That address is only across town, Mr Wallace. I can deliver it personally tonight for you on my bicycle and you can be sure it will be opened first thing in the morning. I can see it's urgent.'

He smiled happily. 'Now wouldn't that be just great. You've made my day, young man, and I want to see you in my office first thing tomorrow morning.'

Next day I got the promotion to part-time personal assistant to Mr Wallace, taking down his letters in shorthand and typing them up in a flash. In the space of one year I was working with him full-time – getting to know how to run a business, working on forecasts and trends, overseeing projects, taking over all marketing functions, handling all his administration, drafting and writing his letters so he only had to sign off.

That's how lucky I was – being in the right place at the right time. But again, I had learned how to write letters from library books and practising. I had learned to take short-hand, I had learned to type efficiently, and I was working late for no extra pay. That's how I was in the right place at the right time with the right skills. I had learned to be lucky.

WHAT GOES AROUND COMES AROUND

It's a saying that's known everywhere: 'What goes around comes around.' Like a carousel. It means that your good deeds will bring you good luck, and when you do others harm you will eventually suffer harm yourself.

In the old days when a wife-beater got beaten up in a street brawl and taken off to hospital, you'd see the wise nods and hear the mutterings 'What goes around comes around.' Likewise, when a charitable couple who were generous to the kids, suddenly got word of a new house for themselves from the Corporation, everyone was over-joyed and wished them well as they left the tenements. 'Lovely people, what goes around comes around.'

In the inner-city community we lived in, where everyone was poor, we didn't really think of ourselves as poor. You see we had no expectations. But we did have great people who cared for each other, who shared with each other. When an expectant mother went into hospital to have a baby the other women of the neighbourhood took care of her family. Getting the kids to school, feeding them, making sure they did their homework. Getting the man of the house off to work too with a good breakfast and a few big sandwiches wrapped in newspaper for his lunch, and a fine plateful of coddle for him when he came home in the evening. This kind of support was reciprocated everywhere.

A perfect example of community support happened in 1957 when I won a Christmas hamper in a grocery store raffle. It arrived about eight o'clock on Christmas Eve and the Ma couldn't believe the size of this wicker hamper. It was five feet long and two feet high and wide. We opened it to see it filled with every kind of Christmas goodies. The Ma looked at me and shook her head. In all the excitement I was probably the only one who heard her mutter 'my lucky child' before she let out a roar.

'Okay, everyone, hands off this stuff. Brian ya rascal, put them chocolates back in there, and Carmel what's that behind your back, come on, back it goes.' She looked at the basket and then pulled out a huge turkey.

'This is for us, the rest is for sharing. Rita, you go tell Missus Sherlock to come over here, and Noel, you do the other side of the street. Tell them we have a Christmas present for everyone.' It took only seconds for the street to come alive. They queued up at the door and one by one the neighbours took their pick from the basket until it was empty. The Ma had kept a cake for the nuns in the convent. Some of the kids did manage to grab a few little trinkets in the mêlée.

So that was sharing in the community I was raised in and the Ma's example has passed to her children. Our family have enjoyed good health and good fortune and we were taught to count our blessings every day and help those who are less well off.

When I was receiving a cheque (for US$25,000) with the Princess Grace Humanitarian Award in Monaco, they asked whom they would make the cheque payable to. 'Make it for Gucci and Armani,' my Jackie said quickly, and when it was completed to the Irish Youth Foundation she piped up, 'Think I'll have to register as Jackie's Children of Need to get a few bob around here.'

Seriously, we have both learned that it's better to give than receive and the Irish Youth Foundation Charity has now raised over forty million dollars since start-up. That money has helped thousands of youth projects all over the island of Ireland. From Bantry Bay to Derry Quay, and from Galway to Dublin town, we have seen thousands of young people get a helping hand onto the ladder of achievement. And the more we help, the more good things happen to us. Through our work with young people we have met Bill and Hillary Clinton in the White House, Tony Blair in Downing Street, Princess Anne in Buckingham Palace, Prince Albert in Monaco. Our network of supporters is spread all over the world because the Irish are everywhere.

No matter how little you have, or how low you may feel, there's always so many who are worse off than you. People who are enslaved, who are maimed, who suffer disease or ill health. We all have a responsibility to help others and I have always found that when you help, good things will come your way. It's a law of nature that Molly Darcy put in her own simple way.

'There's a lot of religion out there son, Catholics, Protestants, Hindus, Muslims and the rest. But all of it comes down to three little words – do unto others.'

IT'S A SMALL WORLD WE LIVE IN

There's a saying that we Irish have that's worth focusing on 'Sure Ireland is only a village'.

Some people think that this reflects our land mass as a very small island on the edge of the Western world. But it's not that at all.

It seems to mean that everyone knows everyone else in Ireland, and that's not really accurate either, with four million of us now having our little bit of it.

But everyone does know someone whom you know, and that's where the expression had true meaning in the old days. Just like when I said to the Kerry man, 'Hello Brian, do you know my friend Senator Coghlan in Killarney?' and he replied he did. Everyone knows someone that you know and that's a fact that builds friendships.

It works better for the Irish than any other nationality, because of our history. For centuries the Irish left their native land. They fled from the yoke of suppression, from massacres and famines, and were exiled when they rebelled against the English invaders. To America, to Australia, to France, all over Europe. Even in Barbados our taxi driver's name was Patrick Clarke, reflecting the emigration of five thousand Irish people exiled to Barbados in the seventeenth century. In fact no matter what country in the world you go to the Irish will have roots in that community. So in that way there's a special meaning for the Irish when we say, 'It's a small world we live in'.

On a broader base, the words have taken on another meaning because of today's technology. Computers, satellites, TV, phones, faxes, email, are all part of the instant information systems that exist today. You can contact anyone anywhere in the world. Pick up the phone, ask the operator to put you through to the First Lady in the White House, and within seconds you'll hear a voice say, 'Hi, this is Teresa, in the First Lady's office, how may I help you today?'

That's how easy it is to contact people and that's why you have a new meaning to the saying 'It's a small world we live in'. And guess what? It's getting smaller all the time.

Air travel gets cheaper and cheaper every day with EasyJet and Ryanair in Europe and Jet Blue in America. Anyone can go around the world in forty-eight hours at a price anyone can afford. It's only one hundred years ago that a record of 'Around The World In Eighty Days' was set by a multi-millionaire with the money to do it. Now our backpacking kids think nothing of skipping off to Australia for a few days.

Cheap travel and contact access brings opportunity. Travelling the world opens your mind to new ideas, new cultures. Go to India and China and see how these economies are making a massive impact on price reduction in the consumer markets. Go to America and see the endless procession of franchises where fortunes will be made. Go to Eastern Europe where hundreds of millions of consumers are emerging into the market place with the support of billions of dollars from the European Union. That's how lucky and privileged you are to be in this world of opportunity. Travel this world and realise the numerous ways you can choose to build your own success in life. Have the confidence to explore new markets, new products and meet new people. That's the glorious opportunity you have to be lucky today because now the world is only a village.

KEEP YOUR COMMITMENTS

Another great way to be lucky is to make commitments to people.

When I meet someone new and get talking to them I always

give them a business card, plus some little gift that I carry around with me. Might be a pair of those fold-up reading glasses, or a new type of pen, or one of those credit card size blue light torches. It's amazing how many people will then email you to say thanks, even though the gifts only cost a few dollars.

Somewhere in the contact time I'll make a commitment to send an article on a topic we've discussed, to get them details of a place they are interested in, to send a brochure of our lovely hotel in Killarney, to send a signed copy of one of my books. And by keeping that commitment I've made a new friend. Life is all about people.

In your day-to-day life, commitments are even more important. You have commitments to yourself and your family. To your employer, to your colleagues, your customers. To enjoy good luck the keeping of those commitments is crucial. People don't always acknowledge the fact that you have kept a commitment but it does register. That's why I have a little notebook with me all the time where I write down the commitments I make to people throughout the day. When you write it down it gets done, and that's how you build your reputation for integrity. Then it always seems that good luck follows integrity.

CREATE THE OPPORTUNITIES

One of the best ways to create opportunities in your life and career is to become an expert at what you do. Be an expert in your chosen subject, know it inside out, be better than your colleagues and competitors, be the man they come to for advice and guidance. That's one way to become a leader and a mentor.

I became an expert in the retail motor industry. I didn't just work twelve hours a day in a car dealership learning all I could about every aspect of the business, I did a lot of other things as well.

Firstly, I invested in monthly subscriptions for every major car magazine published in Ireland, England and America. I read them avidly. I was up to speed on the car trends, knew the progress of the different car manufacturers, which were the hot cars and which were the lemons that bombed out. Saw the spy pictures of the cars of the future.

Secondly, I went to the annual car shows in England and eventually America. Saw the new models months before they arrived in Ireland.

Thirdly, I got myself on the Executive Committee of the Society of the Irish Motor Industry (SIMI) while I was still in my teens. I was in the office at half past one in the afternoon preparing the payroll analysis for wages payout the next day. The phone rang and it was the boss, Mr Wallace, looking for the finance director who was out at lunch. Mr Wallace explained to me that there was a SIMI meeting at 2.15 p.m. which he couldn't make. He needed someone to attend on his behalf to make a Yes vote on an important meeting. 'I can do that for you Mr Wallace, I'll head off right now.'

I was only a seventeen-year-old kid and I found myself at the formidable council table at the SIMI, listening to the discussion on the proposal to have two new executive staff to take over the administrative duties which were then carried out on a voluntary basis. I took the opportunity to introduce myself to the upper echelons of the Irish motor industry. Representing Mr Wallace of Walden Ford, I gave a short but passionate speech on the need for a Yes vote. The action would give impetus and professional support to our industry in the years of growth ahead of us.

Immediately after I sat down, the president commented that there had been enough talk about the proposal, that a youngster still wet behind the years had clarified the need for a Yes vote in a few short sentences. The vote was carried unanimously and many of the people attending came over to shake my hand. The boss was delighted to hear the good news the next day and told me I was to continue as the permanent member of SIMI in his place.

Lucky again? Yes, but that's how I made my own luck. I had a quick bowl of soup for lunch that day so I was available when the phone rang. It was an opportunity and I grabbed that opportunity with both hands when I told the boss, 'Yes, I can do it.' That's how I got the chance at a young age to rub shoulders with the powerbrokers of the motor trade. Stephen O'Flaherty, the first man to take the Volkswagen franchise from Germany after the war when the experts said no one would ever buy a German car again. He got VW, Audi and Mercedes franchises and built an empire that is one of the wealthiest dynasties in Ireland today. Con Smith from Cavan who got the French brands − Renault, Citroën and Peugeot. A dynamic entrepreneur who created one of Ireland's foremost conglomerates, he was a leader of the Irish delegation negotiating our entry into the Common Market (EU). He died tragically, a young forty-two year old, with fifteen Irish businessmen on the way to a final meeting in Brussels. Their plane crashed at Heathrow Airport in 1972 killing all on board.

Attending bi-weekly meetings, and remembering Molly's advice, I looked, I listened, I said little and I learned. When I did choose to make a point I made sure I knew the subject matter inside out and I quickly got the reputation of being on the ball. That led to my appointment as the Honorary Treasurer and I served in the top echelons of SIMI for many decades. Being well thought of by the top people in your field is a sure way to opportunity.

I created the opportunity of buying Renault Ireland by building a strong relationship with Paddy Hayes, the managing director of Ford Ireland. As Chairman of the Ford Dealer Association, I would be in close contact with Paddy and later I had his support in opening my own dealership, Fairlane Ford. So when Paddy moved as CEO of Waterford Crystal (who owned Renault Ireland) and decided to sell the Renault company he put me on his list of possible buyers. Was it just luck that I ended up owning Renault Ireland? Well, the answer to that comes in another story about when I was negotiating the deal. We had the financials agreed with the vendors and all that remained was for Renault to approve me as their representative for Ireland. Two previous aspiring buyers had fallen at this last hurdle.

It would be fair to say that the Renault executives in France were sceptical about giving their beloved brand to a Ford Dealer even if I did have thirty years of experience in the business. So I identified the main player in the panel of judges – the Export Director Pierre Hermann. We talked for a while and I quickly discovered he had spent time with Renault in America where the company had sold a dying business to Lee Iacocca, of Chrysler fame. I knew the whole history of Renault in the USA and we spent a long time discussing the pros and cons and the might-have-beens. Hindsight is a great thing.

We got to discussing how we could review Renault in the Irish car market and I gave Pierre a running commentary of statistics, positioning, the strengths and weaknesses of Renault, how we could create marketing opportunities, dealer network improvements, and how we could implement a cost reduction programme and an innovative plan to resurrect the fortunes of Renault in Ireland.

He eventually stood up abruptly and held out his hand. 'That's enough Monsieur Cullen, you are our man. You know more about this car business than anyone I have ever met. The Renault franchise for Ireland is yours. Good Luck.'

Pierre knew he had met an expert, and all my learning, my time investment, my hard work, my passion for the car business, had finally paid off. Yes, I was lucky but luck is opportunity meeting preparation.

BRICKS CAN BE LUCKY

Glencullen Holdings is the umbrella company that now controls my business empire. I am the Chairman and one hundred per cent shareholder and while the primary business is the Renault Car Franchise for Ireland we have many other interests. Our second biggest company is Glencullen Properties and it's important to realise that everyone who goes into business for themselves will always be in the property business.

The giants like GE, Microsoft and Dell employ thousands of people in any one of their huge plants and office blocks. The tiny units of Starbucks and Subway have thousands of properties, opening a new one every day around the world. In between you have the McDonald's and the KFC chains who buy one acre lots and now have prefabricated building units that enable them to build and open a new premises in seven days.

No matter what business you go into for yourself be aware of property needs and potential. The small unit franchises work on a lease rental basis that minimises the capital investment so they can keep rolling out franchises. All the eating chains know the success mantra is simple. It's about location, location, location.

I learned that principle as a ten-year-old on the streets of Dublin when I was selling flowers.

Where is the best place to sell flowers? Well, as a part-timer it's at a graveyard on Sunday mornings. Then I discovered that every evening the best place to be was outside a Maternity Hospital, where I also learned another business principle – the elasticity of price.

On the street during the day, flowers were a hard enough sell with only one in every few hundred passers-by interested in the flowers. But every single person going into a maternity hospital was a customer. The demand was high and the supply was limited to the amount of flowers I could fit in the kids' pram.

So the bunch of flowers that I would sell for a pound on the street could stretch to two or three pounds each to the eager fathers going to see their new babies.

Of course, that's all changed today with Interflora and 1–800-Flowers able to deliver anywhere in the world, within hours – but it now costs $50 a bunch. See, they are the guys who came up with a way to do it better!

So the positioning of a retail outlet is crucial and fifty yards from a busy street can mean the death knell for a business. By contrast, the McDonald's chain look for easy drive-in access off a major roadway and preferably at a roundabout or junction where the traffic slows down. The big manufacturing plants head for suburbia where the workers live, or the rural areas with workers bussed in from the surrounding town. Their locations are usually driven by the millions of dollars in grant-aid offered by Governments to generate employment. Property in a good location will always rise in value and whatever business you are in you are also in the property appreciation business and that has to be managed.

The first business property I bought in 1974 for $30,000 made $78,000 when I sold it in 1978. Wow, I made more on the property than I did in the business in that four years. A property I bought in 1978 for $90,000 now has a value of six million dollars. Our head office property was bought in 1988 for $500,000 and will make six million dollars today. It's usually better to buy on a mortgage rather than rent when you need a good location. Mortgage repayments are about the same as renting but you will own a valuable asset after the mortgage period ends. On the other hand, renting allows you to expand faster because you don't have the mortgage liability on your balance sheet, while rent can be written off as a business expense. Our property company will very soon overtake our car business in annual profits.

No matter what business you go into, remember you're also in the property business. So take a close look at the options, and get the best tax advice before you lock into the deal. You will always be lucky in business when you pay attention to location, location, location.

MAKE YOURSELF AVAILABLE

One great secret of being lucky is to make yourself available. That's what happened for me when Mr Wallace walked in at seven thirty on that evening. My typing skills would have been useless if I hadn't been there to give him a demonstration that was the cornerstone of my business career. I was there, I was available, because I always went into work an hour or two before the posse. And I stayed for an hour or two after they left. No, I didn't get paid extra for working extra hours, but it was in those hours I was learning the business.

You see, that's the time when the good guys are around. Not just the movers and shakers at executive level but the little guys in our business, like the petrol pump guy, Jimmy Ryan, whom I worked with helping out in the early morning rush pumping gas. The drivers got to know me, liked my style, and that filtered back to the boss.

Sometimes I'd help out in service reception, taking in the cars for service and repairs. The customers liked my enthusiastic approach and the service advisors appreciated the help to clear the early morning rush. And I was learning all about the problems customers have with their cars and figuring out better ways for us to handle and even prevent those problems. I was learning how a smile and a sympathetic approach defused some of the hot tempered situations, because the service reception in a busy car dealership is one big cauldron of complaints.

No one ever comes in to us to say 'Morning guys, isn't it a great day. I just dropped in to say hello and tell you that my car is going absolutely prefect.'

That happens in other retailers: 'My hairdo was terrific. He loved the new dress. The new suit is just fantastic and I need some ties to match.'

No, in a car dealership it's the new car showrooms where all the glamour and goodness is. The only time the service guys see a customer is when there's a problem. So that's a great school for learning to handle problems, and I learned that when you sort out the problem the customer is delighted, probably happier than if the car never had a problem. The intention always is to exceed expectations, fix it quicker than you promised, and get it right first time.

At the back of the shop I also learned about the basic mechanics of a car. Change oil, fix punctures, and engine tune-ups were the simple things I could handle, but I also watched the technicians do the engine overhauls and gearbox reconditioning. So all that time invested gave me a grounding in the business. Which gave me another quantum leap in my career.

Late one evening, Mr Wallace called me into his office and asked me to inspect a car parked on the forecourt. He wanted a used-car appraisal to evaluate a trade-in for a friend. I picked up a pre-printed appraisal form and walked around the car noting the damage marks, the tyres that needed replacing. I inspected the interior where the rear seat upholstery was badly torn and a door lock broken. I took the car for a two minute drive around the block and noted the brakes needed attention, the radio was broken, and there was a bad wheel-bearing whine from the front wheel on the passenger side. I took the completed form up to the boss, who said thanks and that was that.

Until some months later when he asked me would I take the position of branch sales manager. 'Certainly,' I replied.

The company accountant was in the office and he said, 'Do you think you have the expertise to handle trade-ins? That's where the profit is in this business.'

Before I could say a word Mr Wallace produced a folder and placed the car appraisal on the desk.

'He can appraise cars all right. He checked this car for me a while back and he spotted a broken radio, torn upholstery, and a worn wheel-bearing that our number one salesman hadn't spotted. Bill has a keen eye for detail, I'm sure he'll be okay for the job.'

So that's how I got my first management job. I had taken the time to learn about the business, I was willing to have a go at anything, I was always, always available. You know in all my eighteen years in Walden Ford. I was never a minute late. Probably punched in fifty per cent more time than I was being paid for. In salary that is, but wasn't I amply rewarded in the end?

If you want to be lucky, keep on learning about the business you're in and become an expert at it. By being around and available you'll get opportunities. That's what I mean by learning to be lucky.

DO IT BETTER

Molly Darcy's advice to me in 1956 on the first morning I was leaving for my new career as a messenger boy in Walden Ford was very simple.

'You know, son, that you are a warrior and you can do anything you believe you can do. This is your big chance and I want you to remember one little thing. It's only three little words son, but it's the best advice I can give you. Do it better. That's all. Do it better. That means if you are asked to sweep the floor sweep it so clean a King could eat his dinner off it. If you are asked to clean windows leave them so clean they won't even know there's a window there. If they send you out to deliver a message, do it and get back so quick they won't even know you've gone. I can promise you that if you follow my advice you'll be seeing things with the owner's eyes.'

Molly Darcy had never gone to school. I had taught her to read, but she had the wisdom of the world. She sprinkled some Holy Water on my head with a little prayer and gave me a hug.

'Now get that big smile on your face, and off you go. You are terrific.'

Looking back to that wet autumn morning, I can still see her shining eyes and mischievous smile. She was sitting on the stool in her kitchen with the enamel mug of shell cocoa beside her, her black shawl still pulled around her shoulders to keep herself warm. And I realise how privileged I was to have such family support.

Such wise guidance and mentoring. Molly was sixty-three years old then, a widowed street fish-seller, and she could give a seminar with priceless pearls of wisdom that still work today. If you apply her advice to your business life, and get things done quicker and better than anyone else, and see things with an owner's eyes, you will be an owner yourself with all the success that brings. **Do it better!**

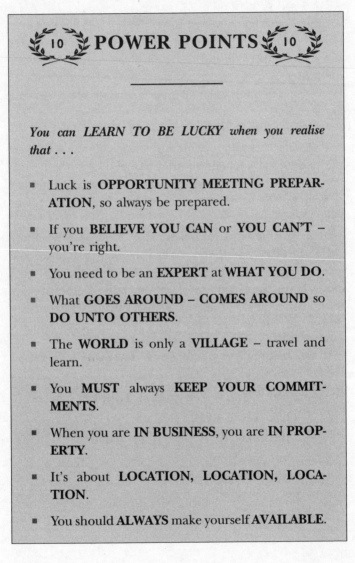

POWER POINTS

You can LEARN TO BE LUCKY when you realise that . . .

- Luck is **OPPORTUNITY MEETING PREPARATION**, so always be prepared.

- If you **BELIEVE YOU CAN** or **YOU CAN'T** – you're right.

- You need to be an **EXPERT** at **WHAT YOU DO**.

- What **GOES AROUND – COMES AROUND** so **DO UNTO OTHERS**.

- The **WORLD** is only a **VILLAGE** – travel and learn.

- You **MUST** always **KEEP YOUR COMMITMENTS**.

- When you are **IN BUSINESS**, you are **IN PROPERTY**.

- It's about **LOCATION, LOCATION, LOCATION**.

- You should **ALWAYS** make yourself **AVAILABLE**.

6

E – ENERGY TO EXCEL

- **You Are What You Eat**
- **Winning Ways**
- **Golden Apples Fitness Plan**
- **Ignite Your Energy**
- **Longevity Can Happen To You**
- **Vitamins Are Vital**
- **Look Younger And Feel Younger**
- **Take Time Out**
- **The Early Bird Gets The Worm**
- **Quit Sleeping**
- **Power Points**

YOU ARE WHAT YOU EAT

Yes, it's so true: our family was never poor, we just had no money.

One precious benefit we had was that we bought and sold fruit, fish and vegetables. So that's what we got to eat in our house. Little did we know then that this was the perfect health and energy diet.

There was never a question of not liking your dinner. If you even hesitated or looked doubtfully at the plate, the Ma would whisk it away saying, 'Well now you mustn't be too hungry today. Your brother will eat this for ya and we'll see if you like it or not tomorrow.' Going without food for twenty-four hours is a great cure for selective eaters.

Breakfast was always porridge on weekdays but on Sunday mornings after Mass it was a fried egg, tomatoes and onions. We got our dinner at lunchtime and in the evenings a mug of tea with a banana sandwich. The dinner menu was simple in our house:

SUNDAY:	corned beef, cabbage and potatoes
MONDAY:	Sunday leftovers reheated with colcannon
TUESDAY:	vegetable stew flavoured with marrowbones
WEDNESDAY:	fresh fish (usually mackerel, cod, or ray) and vegetables
THURSDAY:	vegetable stew (same as Tuesday)
FRIDAY:	fish (same as Wednesday)
SATURDAY:	rabbit and vegetable stew

We all learned to love our carrots, broccoli, turnips, cabbage, sprouts, and cauliflowers, and we had bananas, apples and oranges to choose from as we headed for school. We know now we had better food than the richest people in Ireland.

There were no burgers, no hot dogs, no fast food, no Cokes, no fat pills to slow us down. And with the Ma's dynamic energy driving the household there were no couch potatoes either – in fact we didn't have a couch! We didn't get much in the way of meat as you can see from the menu. The rabbits on Saturday came at a very low price from a friend of the Ma's in the market.

Molly Darcy lived to be one hundred years old on a similar diet and spent most of her life out on the streets selling her fruit and fish in all seasons. The Irish winters are wet and cold and yet I cannot remember Molly with flu or an ailment – except when she fell down the stairs and broke her hip. In her last year she was as lucid and as talkative as any of us, leading the discussions on the latest political scandals.

No Parkinson's, no Alzheimer's, no strokes, no cancers. We talked a lot about that and I came to accept and adopt some of the basic principles that Molly had embraced. Today at sixty-three years old I've never had an ailment, never spent an hour in bed sick, never lost an hour from work through illness and I don't do colds or flu. I am blessed with good health, thank God!

WINNING WAYS

Good health isn't a big secret. Let me remind you of the basic principle of health and energy: it's the simple precept of eating lots of fruit, fish and vegetables. Apart from the great goodness in these foods they are so easy for your body to digest, to absorb the nutrients, to build up your energy and strengthen your immune system.

Compare that with a steak and chips. Yes, the steak has protein but also fat and, worse still, it absorbs valuable energy in digesting it. Did you ever wake up jaded after eating a big sirloin steak the night before? Your body is exhausted after spending the night digesting a huge lump of meat. The fries are full of animal fat, which is a big no-no as it clogs your arteries, so common sense tells you which are the healthier foods to eat.

When it comes to drinking the old common sense applies too. Our home was a dry house – no alcohol. The Ma, the Da, and Molly Darcy were all teetotallers. As lifetime members of the Catholic Pioneers, they abstained from alcohol and I don't believe any one of them was ever in a pub in their lives.

I tell the story of when Molly was in the nursing convent for the last few years of her life. In the cold winter months I'd bring her a bottle of Lucozade. Uncapping the bottle at home, I would drop in a large whiskey, to give some warmth and nourishment to her tired body. She loved it.

'Your Lucozade is only lovely son. Warms me right down to me toes. Will you tell your brothers where you get it? The stuff they bring me is like coloured water.' Everything in moderation, including moderation.

The basic foundation for energy and longevity is healthy food habits and keeping your drinking to a moderate level. I kept my vow of abstinence from alcohol until I was well into my thirties and I firmly believe that this was the cornerstone of my business success. Too often I saw pals and colleagues staying out of work sick – really suffering from hangovers. Or coming to work with sore heads and unable to focus. In the car sales business you had to be on your toes all day every day so I was always ahead of the posse. Being a non-drinker didn't stop my social life and I could still go to parties and enjoy the fun drinking my favourite Taylor Keith lemonade.

I shouldn't have to even mention smoking or drugs but I was lucky enough to bypass these two killers. The damage caused to your health by smoking is well documented but there are many methods to help kick the habit and it takes courage and determination to give up cigarettes. But the best solution is not to start smoking at all.

As for drugs, well the devastation they cause is all around us and I deplore how the celebrities in our society refer to some substances as 'recreational drugs'. If you're doing drugs you're doing damage – to yourself and your loved ones. And they are guaranteed to take you right down to the depths of despair. You don't need 'uppers' or stimulants to get to peak performance. You need a strong mind in a healthy, energised body. We've covered the healthy bit so let's have a look at how to really energise your mind and your body.

I developed the habit of regular exercising. So let me show you how you too can give a huge lift to your energy levels by using a simple daily exercise programme. You don't need to join a gym for a thousand dollars. You don't need to buy a lot of expensive equipment. You just need to have the determination to commit yourself to doing the routine every day. Ingrain it as a habit from which a healthy lifestyle and endless energy will flow.

As an early riser I do my Golden Apples Fitness Plan first

thing when I get out of bed. It kick-starts my day and I firmly believe that getting invigorated and the blood pumping in the early morning is the best way to start and will let you easily cope with the challenges and stress that each day brings.

But if you can't fit it in then for domestic reasons, the evening when you get home is fine. In fact the boost it gives after a hard day's work is just as invigorating, and will take you away from flopping on the couch to watch the TV.

Energy is the key to enthusiastic performance and exercise is the core of energy so let's go now with the Golden Apples Fitness Plan!

GOLDEN APPLES
FITNESS PLAN
FLEXIBILITY WARM-UP

Warm-Up A: Full Arm Swings
20 Forward Circles
20 Backward Circles
Build Up To 3 Repetitions Each Way

Warm-Up B: Trunk Turning
Legs Apart, Arms Shoulder High
Turn Right Through 90° To Face Sideways
Return Face Front and Repeat 10 Times
Turn Left Through 90° To Face Sideways
Return To Face Front, Repeat 10 Times
Build up to 3 Repetitions On Each Side

Stretches C: Side Stretches
Legs Apart
Lean Left, Left Hand Down Calf, Right hand on head
And Pulse 10 Times
(Push Fingers Down 3 Inches)
Lean Right, Hand Down Calf, Left hand on head
And Pulse Ten Times
Build Up to 3 Repetitions On Each Side

Stretches D: Upright Toe Touching
Legs Together, Knees Straight
Fingers on Knees
Stretch Down To Touch Toes
Pulse Down 10 Times
Stand Up Right
Build Up To 3 Repetitions,
Going Lower All The Time

GOLDEN APPLES
FITNESS PLAN
BUM AND TUM EXERCISES

Floor Exercise E: Sitting Toe Touches
Sitting on Floor
Legs Straight Together In Front
Stretch Fingers To Toes (No Knee Bend)
Pulse Forward 10 Times and Relax Upright
Build To 3 Repetitions Stretching More
Each Week

Floor Exercise F: Crunches
Lying on Floor
Knees up, Hands on Thighs
Raise your Head and Stretch your Hands up to the Knees
Back Stays on Floor
Pulse 5 Times and Lower Head to Floor
Repeat 10 Times and Relax
Build up to 5 Repetitions

Floor Exercise G: Bum Raising
Lying on Floor, Knees Bent Up
Raise Bum Off The Ground
While Opening & Closing Knees
Repeat 20 Times and Relax
Build Up To 3 Repetitions

Floor Exercise H: Leg Raises
Lying Flat On Floor Legs Straight Out In Front
Raise Both Legs Together 12 Inches Off Floor
Part Feet (30 Inches) And Bring Together
Repeat 10 Times Without Lowering
Part Feet Up/Down (12 Inches)
Repeat 10 Times and Lower
Take 10 Second Rest and Build Up To 3 Complete Repetitions

GOLDEN APPLES
FITNESS PLAN
STRENGTH EXERCISES
Using A 5 Kilo (or 10 lb) Weight In Each Hand

Standing Exercise I: Side Lifts
Lift Hands sideways To Shoulder Height
And Lower To Side
Repeat 10 Times
Build Up To 3 Repetitive Cycles

Standing Exercise J: Curls
Curl Forearms Forward
And Lower
Repeat 10 Times
Build Up To 3 Repetitive Cycles

Standing Exercise K: Overheads
Lift Hands Forward To Shoulders
Push Fully Overhead And Lower
Repeat 10 Times
Build Up To 3 Repetitive Cycles

Standing Exercise L: Chest Pulls
Lift Hands Forward To Shoulders
Push Fully Sideways And Lower
Repeat 10 Times
Build Up To 3 Repetitive Cycles

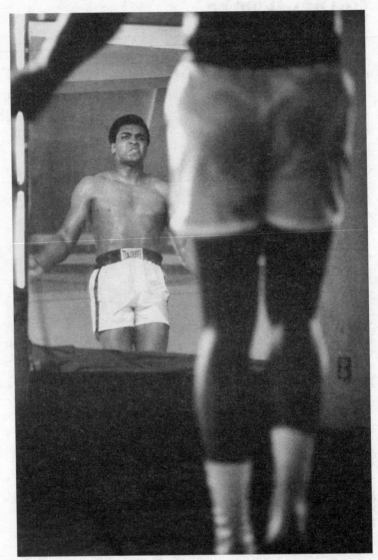

Muhammad Ali, skipping

GOLDEN APPLES FITNESS PLAN

THE XTRA MILE

These exercises may look easy to any fit young person but you just have a go at the maximum repetitions of each. Then go the Xtra Mile with ten minutes skipping. Then let's see you do the 100 push-ups. Then tell me it's a breeze like you first thought. If so, you are an athlete and you are terrific. For everyone else, the Golden Apples Fitness Plan is a platform for energy.

The Stretches give your body flexibility and a great sense of wellbeing that will keep you nimble into your middle-aged seventies.

The Crunches will build up your stomach muscles and with it your confidence and your determination. It feels terrific to have a flat belly, as Napoleon knew when he said, 'An Army marches on its stomach' – that's where the guts and courage are.

The Small Weights build lean muscular power. Better still it develops bone density and will fight the onset of osteoporosis, which is especially important for women.

This Xtra Mile bit is the important bit, for the cardiovascular system. After you finish the weights, go the Xtra Mile with an aerobic finish.

You do Ten Minutes Skipping
Starting with an Easy 2 or 3 Minutes
And Build it Up to 10 Minutes
If You Don't Have a Skipping Rope
Just Pretend You Have it in Your Hands
And Skip with an Invisible Rope

This finisher will get the blood pumping and some sweat on your brow – and it's time then for your shower and you are ready for all the day's challenges. One last thing about the shower. Use a body scrub. Get an exfoliating brush and give your body a good strong brushing using a nice fragrant body lotion. This takes a lot of toxins out of your system and it is also a terrific energiser.

Let's take an overview of how you can use just 25 minutes a day to focus on health and energy

1st	The Arm Swing Warm-ups	A, B
2nd	The Stretches	C, D, E, F
3rd	The Belly & Bum Toners	G, H
4th	The Lean Muscle Builder	I, J, K, L
5th	The Xtra Mile – Skipping	
6th	The Body Scrub Energiser	

Develop the habit of doing the exercises every day. It is not what you do or when you do it – it's *that* you do do it!

Unlike the Lord on the Sabbath, you don't miss a day. It's every day, without fail, no excuses. So you do it every day until it becomes as automatic as cleaning your teeth.

If you travel a lot you can still do your routine. Instead of your weights, do half push-ups off the wash unit in the bathroom – start with twenty and build up. Push-ups are an all-over body toner. They tighten your bum, your belly, your thighs and your shoulders all in one exercise. Start with half push-ups on the third last step on your staircase. When you can do seventy come down to the second last step and when you can do sixty it's down to the last step. You do fifty on the last step until you are strong enough to do fifty full push-ups off the flat floor.

That's a programme that would take three months per step to finish. So after twelve months you'd be a fifty push-up athlete. And in another twelve months you'd do the ton. Yes, one hundred push-ups in a two-year programme, and you know two years goes by very fast. If you really want to be fit this exercise is the number one. This is the exercise of a real warrior.

At weekends and on nice evenings take a walk. Stretch those legs and pull some fresh air into your lungs. Walk twenty minutes out and twenty minutes back. Make it a brisk power walk and you'll do two miles.

Exercise is the core of energy. You are releasing those little happy chappies called endorphins into your bloodstream and they pump energy through your system. They make your blood tingle. You feel strong and confident. Your brain will buzz with ideas. You feel a zest for living. You can take on the world. You are a peak performer. You are terrific.

IGNITE YOUR ENERGY

HEALTHY EATING

- Stick to fruit, vegetables, fish, salads, chicken
- Power juice for breakfast – fruit smoothies
- Drink six glasses of water a day, the colder the better
- No, No, No, to chips, fries, burgers, hotdogs, red meat, popcorn, potato crisps, dairy products
- No, No, No to biscuits, cookies, cakes, breads, sausages

ALCOHOL

- It ages you, kills brain cells, and slows you down
- Red wine, in moderation, is good
- More than 15 drinks a week is too much

SMOKING

- It kills you, gives you wrinkles and sucks the vital nutrients from your body
- Gives you cancer, heart attacks, strokes, and clogs your arteries
- If you do smoke – get the help to quit
- If you don't you are terrific – don't ever start

DRUGS

- Short-term highs, for a lifetime of misery
- Don't go there

HEALTH

- The Golden Apples Fitness Plan
- 25 minutes a day to be a winner
- Look great, feel terrific
- Gives you strength and confidence
- Adds 10 years to your life

VITAMINS

- The Health Pack – ACES. The Cancer Fighters
- The Energy Pack – CQ10 & L Carnitine. The Vitality Builders

POSITIVE THINKING

Don't forget your daily affirmations every morning and get the happy chappies going with a big smile.

LONGEVITY CAN HAPPEN FOR YOU

In Roman days life expectancy was about twenty-seven years. If you made it past thirty you were old. At the turn of the nineteenth century lifespan averages were up to forty-five years. Today we can expect to make seventy-five years, and we have plenty of eighty and ninety year olds around. The oldest person in Ireland is one hundred and eight and there was a Japanese lady who made it to one hundred and twenty years old.

Some people of ancient times did achieve a ripe old age, like Socrates, the Greek philosopher who is reputed to have made the one hundred mark. St Kevin of Glendalough lived a definitive one hundred and twenty years from AD 498 to AD 618 and Michelangelo made it to eighty-nine years of age. Today, with the latest information on nutrition, we know that there is no biological reason why we cannot live to be a hundred and twenty years old like St Kevin.

Most people die of illness, disease and accidents – not from old age. The secret of longevity is to avoid those life takers. You need to practise the habits of longevity, some of which I have already shared with you. You have to take responsibility for your health by having a fitness plan that exercises your body. By keeping active to exercise your mind. By having a healthy lifestyle of eating and drinking and stopping polluting yourself with cigarettes.

Of course, we will grow old, but we don't have to become weak and sick and feeble. We can postpone middle age into our seventies by taking charge of our bodies, by adopting a positive outlook.

Yes, it's back to positive thinking again. It doesn't matter how old you are now, you can turn the clock back by simply thinking and believing you will live to be a hundred.

That's right, just start planning your life on that basis. Forget about this routine that you are middle aged at forty, retired and out to grass by sixty, getting the old age pension by sixty-five. Yes, even the Government have you convinced you're old at sixty-five so tell them to stick it. At sixty-five you can still make the rest of your life the best of your life. You can still be virile, active and bursting with vitality. You can still be planning Wow projects and enjoying achievements you may have thought were long past.

Get your mind thinking young and your body will respond. Reject the thinking that it's normal for your joints to start aching, for your belly to hang like a sack of spuds, for the ageing process to overwhelm you. The day you look in the mirror, pull in your belly, and push your chest out and say 'I am terrific' twenty times will start a new world for you. Believe that you will live a long healthy life and your mind will set those happy chappies in motion and give you the strength you need to make your thoughts a reality.

Start today by implementing some part of the Golden Apples Fitness Plan and the results in just a few days will amaze you. Start today taking more care of your appearance, change your hairstyle, get a new suit, get that smile on your face and some pep in your step. This is the only life you are going to get. Enjoy it!

At sixty-three years of age I feel I'm in my prime. We don't have to do middle age. With a proper lifestyle you can make it healthily to a hundred and enjoy every bit of it – but you have to give the Good Lord a hand. Many people try to destroy themselves – smoking, alcohol abuse, drugs, unhealthy food, no exercise, stress, sun-tanning skin damage, negative and anxious mindsets.

Most of us are given a glorious healthy body and don't appreciate it until we suffer ill health. Molly Darcy made me aware of what a privilege it was to be strong and fit and healthy in a world of so much illness and people suffering from diseases and handicaps. 'Never complain son. Once you can hop out of bed in the morning – every day is a great day!'

VITAMINS ARE VITAL

The food we eat today is getting refined and processed with more of the vital nutrients being lost along the way. We don't have the time to examine the labels on cans and packages. Even if you have the time, the writing is so small you would need a magnifying glass to read it. There are so many different ways to confuse us that you would need a science degree to figure it all out. So let's keep it simple.

Eat fresh fruit, vegetables, grilled fish (no batter) and salads as primary food, and make sure you use only olive oil for cooking – no animal fat.

Keep away from burgers, hot dogs, French fries (chips), cakes, crisps, popcorn, biscuits and the hearty Irish breakfast because those sausages, bacon and puddings are loaded with fat. You should also be aware of the cancer dangers in smoked or barbecued food. Outside of that, everything in moderation and you've a fairly healthy diet.

But you need to add vitamin supplements to make up for the nutrition loss in today's food supplies. Not just to keep your energy level high but to strengthen your immune system. A strong immune system keeps colds and flus away and protects you against the strokes, cancers, heart attacks and other diseases that are killing so many people in our modern world.

On top of my healthy eating I take two portions of vitamins a day:

Health Pack – It's the Aces, that's vitamins A, C, E and
selenium:

Vitamin A: An antioxidant, a cancer protector. I take 10,000 IU of Beta-Carotene every day.

Vitamin C: The best immune protector of all, soluble tablets, dropped in water. I take 1000 mg twice a day.

Vitamin E: For eyes and skin care. I take 400 IU per day

Selenium: A great antioxidant. I take 50 mcg per day

The Aces will build up your immune system and protect you from all the usual colds, flus and fatigues that go around. They also build up your body's protection against the ravages of cancer and heart attacks, which are the two biggest killers in our society. Protect yourself, get strong inside as well as outside!

Energy Pack – Two little supplements for you to add to your health vitamins:

CQ10:   A big energy booster as well as a cancer protector. I take 50 mg a day.

L-Carnitine: Works terrifically with CQ10. I take 500 mg a day.

This is a great pair of natural energy boosters that will power you through the challenges and stress of your day. You'll feel you can go through a brick wall.

Take your health and energy packs every day and you will feel revitalised and dynamic.

Another Food Tip – Water. Drink as much as you can but at least six glasses a day. Don't drink tap water unless you have a filter system. You can buy a water distiller unit and distilled water is best, but bottled water or from the cooler is fine. That helps all the other food habits to work more easily and replaces the fluids you are losing in your new go-go lifestyle! And the colder the water is the more toxins it will flush out!

Last Food Tip – Fruit Smoothies. The power juices. I bought my first fruit grinder thirty years ago. Every morning I grind together grapes, pear, apple, strawberries, bananas and raspberries with fruit juice or water and have two big glasses of power juice for breakfast. I even have a grinder in the office for my timeout breaks. It's an easy way to get powerful energy nutrients into your system and those fruit smoothies are full of cancer-beating antioxidants and flavenoids that will ignite your immune system to warrior levels!

Make these changes in your lifestyle and you can increase your life by ten years and even twenty years. Your body recreates itself every six months, so change your habits and you'll have a new, vigorous, healthy, energetic you in a few short months.

As Molly Darcy often said, even in her nineties, 'We all want to go to Heaven, but not yet!' Life is precious and you too can live healthily until 100. Keep to the Golden Apples Fitness Plan for ten days, and you will feel re-energised and full of health and vigour.

You're On The Way To
A New You

Two Pals Celebrate Bloomsday – Tommy Sherlock & Bill Cullen

LOOK YOUNGER AND FEEL YOUNGER

The Golden Apples Fitness Plan is your roadmap to the Land of Youth. It will make you feel younger. Exercising will firm up your body, tone up your muscles and give you flexibility. You will have renewed vigour, you will lose weight, you will flush out the toxins and the dancing happy chappies will have you surging with energy. You will sleep easily and wake up fresh as a daisy. You will walk faster and hop up the stairs without a bother. You will really believe you are terrific.

All this energy will put a real pep in your step. So let's make sure your visage and your image comes with you. You will feel younger and you want to look younger too don't you?

First thing on the look-younger agenda is the sun, the life giver that is at the centre of the universe. The god that was once believed to be the core, the creator of all things. We know that sunshine brings life to flora and fauna and warms our old bones too. But when it gets direct access to our skin it's a killer. Hospital nurses will tell you that no matter how wizened and wrinkled the face gets, the skin on your bum will stay white and soft as a baby's. Why? Because the sun never gets at your bum. It's protected from the cradle to the grave.

You have to protect yourself from the damage that the sun's ultraviolet rays cause to your face and hands by using a sunscreen. Not just on the beach and by the pool, or on the golf course – but every day in your normal activities. Just look at what sunrays do to your couch covers at home – they make them wrinkled and faded. Every day, those rays get at your skin, drying out the moisture and zapping the collagen. So use a moisturiser that has a sun protection factor of at least 15 (SPF15) every day and on the days you are outdoors make sure it's at least SPF20.

The great skin protection secret I can share with you comes from the Dublin street sellers. They were out on the streets all day in all types of weather long before sun protection was heard of. But they always sprinkled water on their faces and hands a few times a day. When the moisturising lotions came out they still sprinkled the water on before applying the lotion.

That's a habit to take on board – every morning rub some water on your face and hands before you rub in some moisturising SPF15. The lotion or cream will trap the water into your skin and make it so much more effective. The younger you start that process the younger you will look for the rest of your life. Clear vibrant skin that will resist the elements can be yours if you take care of it.

The second attack on your face comes from cigarettes. They contain more than four hundred toxic substances and although every cigarette box carries the slogan Smoking Kills, cigarettes are still consumed by the billions.

We know how the sun is an external attacker causing wrinkles and melanoma cancer. Cigarettes are the internal killer. They are at the root of practically every disease you can think of – but they are damaging your skin too. They dry up your juices and kill off the collagen that keeps your skin firm. In a room of forty year olds it's easy to spot the smokers.

To look younger protect your face and hands from the sun and do not smoke cigarettes. If you adopt the habits of the Golden Apples Fitness Plan you get the benefit of the Health and Energy Packs which are powerful anti-ageing activists. The fruit and vegetables you are eating will bring a glow to your skin and a sparkle to your eyes. You can look ten to fifteen years younger than your biological age.

Take a look at the picture on page 138. That's me on the right. Do I look sixty-three years old? So the programme has worked for me, and it will work for you too. No matter how much you have let yourself go, once you *start now* you can take ten years off your appearance in a few short weeks.

TAKE TIME OUT

Now that we've learnt how to energise ourselves, it's important to know how to keep that energy going. The energy can run out if we push it too hard, so learn to take a little rest during the day. If you are sitting at a desk, get up at least every couple of hours and take a walk around. Grab that glass of water and talk to Mary about the movies or Tommy about the football match. If you're on your feet all day then have a sit down for ten minutes every couple of hours. Have a glass of water, close your eyes for a few minutes, slow the motor down. Focus your mind on a special tranquil memory. You're sitting on a beach hearing the waves wash in beside you.

It's our eyes that stimulate our brain most of all, so close them down and the brain relaxes; that lets the energy regather and away you go again. These short breaks recharge the batteries and kick-start your energy. Don't rest or sleep on these breaks for longer than twenty minutes or lassitude sets in and you'll feel tired instead of refreshed. So it's ten to twenty minutes max., okay?

The man who discovered the principle of resting at work was a Scotsman – Andrew Carnegie – who became the richest man in the world. He was a foreman on the railroads in America, building the railway from coast to coast. He became aware that the working teams laid 300 feet of track in the morning seven to one o'clock six-hour shift, but only 160 feet of track in the two to eight o'clock afternoon six-hour shift. A total of 460 feet a day. The men were full of vigour in the morning but got tired in the afternoon and productivity dropped by nearly fifty per cent. Carnegie tried some new shift rosters and eventually got the ideal balance. He gave the teams a twenty minute break every two hours and shortened the working day by one hour. The men were now only working nine hours and forty minutes instead of the original twelve hours – for the same wage. But track laying *increased* to 700 feet a day. Magic! For the same pay the men worked twenty per cent less time but productivity increased by fifty per cent. That's a win-win result. That's how regular rest breaks will refresh your energy.

Carnegie went on to establish the Pullman luxury railway coaches, then the US Steel Company, making all the steel for the booming railway construction and car companies of America. He was a billionaire in the early twentieth century. So take a tip from the canny Scot and take a rest before you get tired.

We are all going full blast in this hassled world we live in. To keep your energy charged up, make sure you take a break from the normal work routine. At least every three months take a week or even a long weekend off and get away from it all. Do something different. A holiday, walking, fishing, gardening, cycling in your own time. Don't flatten the battery, take time out to recharge the system.

THE EARLY BIRD GETS THE WORM

Resting brings up another important aspect of energy and that's sleep. And this is the subject of many proverbs, such as Molly Darcy's favourite:

> Early to bed and early to rise
> Is the way to be
> Healthy, wealthy and wise

But how many hours' sleep do we really need? We are supposed to sleep when it's dark but that varies with the seasons or the country you live in. We all have different metabolisms and I'm a lark who loves getting up early while Jackie is an owl who loves staying out late.

Of course, I love a late-night party but a couple of nights a month is fine! One thing is sure and that is that the body prefers a consistent pattern. Sleep is when our cells regenerate, when the muscles and the brain rest. And the question remains – how much sleep do we really need? On this one I go against the tide. I don't believe in the eight to nine hours story.

My mother only got three to four hours' sleep a night, knitting and darning, and washing and ironing, and minding babies into the wee hours. And off again at half five in the morning after a few hours dozing, sometimes falling asleep in her chair without getting to bed at all. So I think it is about habit, conditioning, being consistent.

I hit the hay most nights around midnight but I'm up always before five o'clock in the morning. No alarm clock anywhere; I just wake up before five and when I wake up I get up and straight into my fitness routine. So I get about four and a half to five hours' sleep a night.

Why get up early? Because it's the best part of the day. No one around. Time to prepare. Review the Plan of Action. Prioritise. Have the power juices. Exercise, shower, shave, dress. Look into the mirror, give myself a big smile and say 'I am terrific' twenty times. I never leave the house without giving Jackie a hug and whispering 'I love you'.

I'm ready to take on the world as I drive up the traffic-free roads before six o'clock. It's habit, it's ingrained, and I feel great. I am ahead of the posse, I'm one up on the other guys, I've got a head-start in the race.

Remember, Molly Darcy told me, 'Sleeping is the nearest thing to dying you'll ever do so don't do too much of it.' Think about that. I did and I'm delighted and excited to be able to hop out of bed every morning.

To reinforce the point, I was at a motivational seminar a few years ago in the huge Orlando Conference Centre. The keynote speaker was Mike Vance, author of *Think Outside The Box* and the late Walt Disney's right-hand man. Mike sauntered onstage, hands in his pockets, looked out at the audience of four thousand people (who had paid $100 a head to hear him) and said, 'I suppose you guys are here to learn the secret of success.'

Yeah, sure, and nods from the floor.

Mike turned his ear to the hall and put his hand on it.

The crowd screamed and shouted, 'Yeah, that's why we're here, we wanna know the secret of success.'

Mike held up his hand. Silence.

He clicked his fingers. The lights went out.

Smoke started to blast from the curtains and ceiling.

Thunder reverberated around the hall, then lightning flashed and a rumbling voice said, 'Here is the secret of success' and two half naked angels descended on a trapeze from the roof, with a large banner hanging from the trapeze. A bolt of lightning hit the banner and two words lit up.

QUIT SLEEPING

Total silence as the stunned audience gazed at the half-clad angels. I mean, we gazed at the banner, and those two words were flashing into our minds.

Mike Vance whispered. 'Any questions?' A big Irishman stood up in the front row. I was given a microphone. 'Mister Vance, my granny told me that for nuthin fifty years ago.'

Silence in the hall.

He looked down at me, gave me a big smile and said, 'Are you a millionaire, son?'

'I am indeed,' I replied and he held his hands wide, looked out over the audience and said, 'Hallelujah – now all you guys know it works.'

Talking afterwards, Mike paraphrased Molly's words when he advised on how to sleep less.

'Put a coffin on your bed, climb in every night and see how long you sleep.'

My own advice to the nine hours a night brigade is to take two minutes a week off your alarm clock and in two years, without ever noticing, you'll be sleeping three hours less every night.

Has my sleeping regime damaged my health in any way? Look at my pictures. At sixty-three I could pass for ten years younger and my business overlaps twenty-five companies with a $400 million annual turnover. I'm a hands-on operator, leading from the front, developing at least two new major projects a month.

I wrote my bestselling autobiography, *It's A Long Way From Penny Apples*, in four weeks, getting up on vacation at four in the morning and writing until two in the afternoon before heading for the holiday activities. All four hundred and eighty pages written with a pen in longhand at twenty-five pages a day.

The best stimulant you can take is a natural personal resource – exercise. Exercising doesn't just give you the physical benefits of conditioning your body. It stimulates your mind as the blood and oxygen pulse through your system. Exercising pumps those natural mood-elevating endorphins throughout your body. These happy chappies give you a natural fix that will last all day.

My fitness plan gives you a simple twenty minute early morning programme that will kick-start your day. It will give you the energy to control your time and let you take it easy. It's not about speed, it's about being in control, working smarter, being effective. Forget speed and let those natural happy chappies make you feel terrific.

So time will tell, and when you gotta go, you gotta go. But it's my intention to get another thirty-five years of work and fun out of this life – with the help of God and a few policemen, of course. I don't see retirement as an option.

'It's better to wear out than rust out' is another of Molly Darcy's sayings that has worked for me.

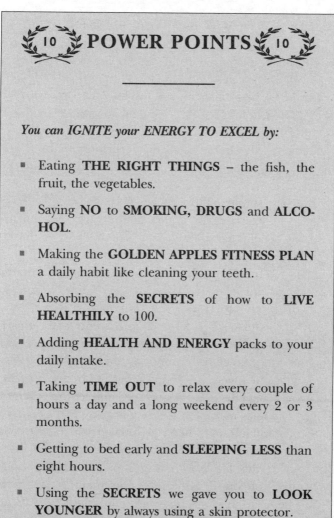

POWER POINTS

You can IGNITE your ENERGY TO EXCEL by:

- Eating **THE RIGHT THINGS** – the fish, the fruit, the vegetables.

- Saying **NO** to **SMOKING, DRUGS** and **ALCOHOL**.

- Making the **GOLDEN APPLES FITNESS PLAN** a daily habit like cleaning your teeth.

- Absorbing the **SECRETS** of how to **LIVE HEALTHILY** to 100.

- Adding **HEALTH AND ENERGY** packs to your daily intake.

- Taking **TIME OUT** to relax every couple of hours a day and a long weekend every 2 or 3 months.

- Getting to bed early and **SLEEPING LESS** than eight hours.

- Using the **SECRETS** we gave you to **LOOK YOUNGER** by always using a skin protector.

- Getting those endorphins – **THE HAPPY CHAPPIES** – pumping naturally through your body.

7

S – SELLING SKILLS TO SUPERCHARGE YOUR SUCCESS

- Nothing Happens Until You Sell Something
- Helping People To Buy
- Give Customers What They Want
- Exceed Expectations
- Take Care Of Your Customer
- Nothing Is Sold Until It's Paid For
- Stand Out From the Crowd
- Teach A Man To Fish
- Selling Anything To Anyone
- Make A Name For Yourself
- A Passion For Service
- Power Points

NOTHING HAPPENS
UNTIL YOU SELL SOMETHING

No matter what business you are in, the product or service has to be sold. No matter how essential your product is, it has to be sold. No matter how much your service is needed, it still has to be sold.

Just think about all the items that we consider essential to our lifestyle today that were only created in the past one hundred years. They would never have sold unless people knew about them, learned how they would improve their life, and then found how they could afford to pay for them. Basic things that we didn't realise we needed like:

Toothbrush	– we used our fingers with a bit of soap
Hairdryer	– we used a towel
Electric bulb	– we used oil lamps and candles
Air conditioner	– we stifled and opened the window
Vacuum cleaner	– we used a sweeping brush
Washing machine	– we used elbow-grease and hand-washed the clothes
Dishwasher	– we used soap and hot water
Car	– the horse was terrific

My point is that someone saw the way to do it better, then went and sold the idea to clients. For most businesses, the idea has to be sold to financial backers first.

In every business today the most important people are the salespeople. Every product and service now has a competitor and the winners aren't always those with the best product. The rewards usually go to the people with the best marketing and selling skills.

The motor industry has hundreds of brands selling tens of thousands of different models. There are too many car manufacturers with too many assembly plants building too many cars. But guess what? Every car that's built gets sold. It's the ones that sell at a profit that will survive.

The retail car market is a warrior's arena for salespeople. In a supermarket or department store customers just walk in, pick up an item, pay for it and walk out. In the car business the customer carefully chooses which dealership he goes into, it's not just the one that's located closest to him.

Customers will spend days driving around, making comparisons, looking for a better deal, because the car business is unique. We trade in your old car, you're spending a lot of money, the trade-in prices vary because every eye forms its own beauty. Good car salespeople have the best selling skills of any business. While the best car salespeople have a degree of innate personality that helps them stand out, we can still train anyone to be terrific in the salesroom.

Every business has a team of people including managers, office people and accountants, but for them nothing happens unless somebody sells something. If we're not selling we won't need accountants to assess the profits, we'll be gone bust. If we're not selling we won't need office people to process the paperwork. If we're not selling, we won't need managers because there's nothing to manage. The guy with selling skills will always have a job because selling is about selling yourself, not just a product.

You become a good salesperson by your ability to develop a rapport with customers, by being sincere, by evoking trust, by exceeding expectations, by knowing your product. Then you're helping people to buy! That's how salespeople sell and that's how they support all the other people in the business. That's why you will always have a good job if you develop your selling skills.

I want everyone in my business to have those selling skills. I want the accounts people to be salespeople so when they handle an accounts query they do it well and sell the customer on our back office services. Many an important customer has been lost by a pompous or discourteous accounts clerk. The telephone person in every team should be a super salesperson because it's at the first point of contact that we can give the customer a happy experience. So make sure you get yourself a warm friendly telephone operator who has a smile in their voice.

Whatever career you choose for yourself you will be a far superior contributor if you have developed your selling skills. Selling skills will enhance your ability to succeed. If you are running your own business, always try to have people with selling skills in every function. People who know how to sell, who have been taught how to sell, how to give the customer a happy experience, how to exceed customer expectations in every facet of your business. That's how you keep customers for life. Realise that the secret of all successful businesses is being able to **identify** customers, to **attract** those customers to your product or service, to **sell** to those customers, to **retain** them, and to do all that at a **profit**. So even though you may have a great product, it's in the sales and marketing areas that the battle is won or lost. So make sure all your people are focused on looking after the customers – it's the customers who pay all our salaries.

HELPING PEOPLE TO BUY

In the old days the humble salesman was pretty low on the totem pole. Going around the frontier towns of America in the new railway trains, they were called 'carpetbaggers' because their samples bags were made of carpet-type material. Many of these carpetbaggers were con artists and tricksters, selling products that didn't work, like snake oil for venereal disease, or promising supplies that never arrived while they skipped off with your money. Then we had the horse-traders who sold horses that were older than they looked or with illnesses that were camouflaged with medicines, or, worse still, horses that had been stolen and their identifying marks covered up with dyes. Too bad if the rain came down!

Then the automobile arrived and with it the car salesmen. In the early days, when Henry Ford brought out his Model T at an incredibly low price thanks to his innovative mass production assembly line, selling cars was easy as demand exceeded supply.

It was in the Great Depression of the 'thirties, the war years of the 'forties, followed by the consumer expansion of the 'fifties in America that the car salesman got a bad name. They got up to all kinds of tricks: selling lemons with worn components dickyed up, turning back mileage odometers, stuffing back axle units with sawdust and selling crash damage cars with cover-up repairs. Yes it was *caveat emptor* – let the buyer beware.

Some years ago I met an American in Killarney named Red Fay who was campaign manager for John Fitzgerald Kennedy in the 1959 USA Presidential Election. That election went to the wire, with Kennedy beating Richard Nixon

JF Kennedy

by a mere 200,000 votes out of an American population of 240 million people. Red Fay told me that the winning thrust he used in the last few days before the election swung it for Kennedy. It was a five-second TV ad, running every half hour, which simply showed a still picture of Nixon. It was an unflattering head shot with Nixon looking truculent, with a very sinister five o'clock shadow.

The voice-over said nine short words with a condemning resonance: 'Would you buy a used car from this man?' Poor ould Nixon was clearly but subtly portrayed as slippery and dishonest. Of course afterwards we found he wasn't called 'Tricky Dicky' for nothing, either.

But as a car salesman now for almost fifty years, I have to say that the profession is unfairly stereotyped. The car

Richard Nixon

salesman today is a trained professional with product knowledge and people skills and in fact he doesn't really sell cars at all. He isn't even always a he, because more and more we have lady sales consultants for the simple reason that we are now **helping people to buy**.

Today's consumers are knowledgeable about what they want, they have done their research on the Internet and won't tolerate a hard sell. Car showrooms nowadays are as comfortable as any department store, with children's play areas, coffee shop, and televised car tests. It's now a very pleasant experience to choose your car, get a trade-in price and a transparent finance deal.

But the selling skill of the sales consultant is still the primary factor in the transaction. People buy from people. You have to establish a rapport with the customer, show a likeable personality, empathise with the customer's concern and let them want to buy from you.

The most important thing you can do in a selling situation is to **pay attention to the customer**. Ask questions and pay close attention to the answers. Don't let yourself be distracted. Keep yourself face-to-face, eyeball-to-eyeball with the customer. Focus on what the customer is saying. Try to understand what she really means. Get behind the words by listening carefully. Don't let your eyes flick away to something else. Let her know that every single word she's saying is important, that you are taking everything in.

That's the first secret of being a good salesperson, don't ever try to sell to the customer. Your whole focus should be on helping people to buy. The way you'll keep a customer for life is to help them to buy the right product at the right price.

GIVE CUSTOMERS WHAT THEY WANT

The secret of having a successful business is to know what your customers want and then give it to them. When you give customers what they want, you'll have lots of customers beating their way to your door. When you give customers what they want, they will tell their friends, who will also beat their way to your door. When customers beat their way to your door they are prepared to pay your price for the product, so you can look after all of them at a profit.

So the question is, what do customers want? In the airline business they used to think that customers wanted to be pampered with food and drink and plush waiting areas and we paid the high price. Since the advent of SouthWest

Airlines, Jet Blue, Ryanair, and EasyJet, we know that what most customers really want is low-cost carriers. These low-cost carriers became lost cost by cutting out all the frills and by having a much faster aircraft turnaround. So you have to be on time and if you miss the plane you have to pay for another ticket. If you want a cup of tea or coffee with a sandwich you pay for it. If you book early you get a low price, if you're a last-minute passenger you pay through the nose. You book online and don't pay any travel agents fees. The check-in team run to departures and double at the gate to keep staff numbers down. Pretty soon you'll be taking hand luggage only because they will be charging you big time for baggage handling – a set of golf clubs is as big and as heavy as an adult so you'll be charged pro rata. The huge number of new air travel customers just want those low cost trips and that's what they will get.

So is low cost the only way forward? Is low cost the template for all business? The answer is absolutely **no**.

The airline business is only selling one thing – a trip from A to B at a great low price and you can compare that cost online in minutes to get the best deal. That doesn't apply to the daily necessities of life.

You buy your daily groceries where you get easy parking and a hassle-free, in and out experience somewhere handy on your daily route.

You buy your other home products at the shopping centre because, again, it's easy to park, there's a great selection of shops, with cinemas and food courts for leisure and entertainment, all under one roof. Price is not a big factor. Do you know the price of a packet of cornflakes, of a new dining-room suite, of a cinema ticket, never mind all the goodies the kids want going to the cinema?

The answer is, no you don't, you just pay. But you do know it's a happy, pleasant experience to go to the shopping centre. That's why millions of people flock to shopping centres all over the world. Shopping has become the world's Number One Leisure Activity.

In most business it isn't about low cost. Pharmaceutical items have no price parameters because when you need it you need it right now. Cosmetics prices are off the wall but so what? You can pay hundreds of thousands of dollars for a Ferrari or a Maybach and the low cost Yugo manufacturers went bust. House prices go from A to Z, and borrowing costs can vary by huge amounts.

The fact is that for most products and services the customer is prepared to pay for a happy, hassle-free experience. That's where to put the customer's focus – on that happy experience. Exceed their expectations and your business will be successful.

So, if you want to be successful, you need to learn how to give customers what they want. Your first customer is your employer and you give them what they want by contributing more than the next guy, by exceeding expectations, by doing things better, by making yourself available and by seeing everything through the owner's eyes.

You take care of the business's customers as if they are friends, giving them a happy hassle-free experience. Selling skills are so important, because people still buy from people, and the more you develop your selling skills the more successful you will be!

EXCEED EXPECTATIONS

In my early career I always exceeded expectations with my enthusiastic approach to every situation. The habit of being an early riser got me into work early. I was so grateful to have a job I liked, I was prepared to work day and night to keep it and get better at it. I watched everything that was going on, eager to learn every aspect of the business. I tried all the time to find better ways to do things. And in eight short years I went from messenger boy to general manager at twenty-two years of age.

How did that happen?

Well, I got the opportunity to sit down with my old boss, Mr Wallace, in later years and I asked him that question.

This was his answer. 'You first made a big impression on me when you typed that letter. So unusual in those days, it showed a very ambitious personality. But the envelope incident was a knockout, do you remember that night Bill?'

I shook my head. 'What envelope?'

'It was a cold winter night that, myself and Missus Wallace were going home from a party. Very late it was, about two o'clock in the morning and going by the dealership we spotted the light on in the office. I pulled in to check it out and found yourself at the desk sorting out two big bundles of envelopes.

'What on earth were you doing in the office at that hour of the night?

'You explained that it was the last day of the month and you always stayed over to prepare the monthly statement accounts to get out to our customers. The quicker I get these out, you said, the sooner we can start phoning customers to pay the bill.

'You also explained that one bundle of envelopes were stamped and you'd deliver them to the post office for mailing. But the other, bigger, bundle you would personally deliver on your bicycle going home, as those customers lived pretty local and we'd save the cost of the postage.

'I was gobsmacked. I went down to my wife and told her we had a kid up there looking after the business better than I did. Staying late into the night on thirty-first December, New Year's Eve, while I was out enjoying myself. That's the fella I want running my business and the sooner the better.'

Little did I realise that my passion to excel in that small way had made such an impact and got me the opportunity to achieve. So when I talk about selling skills, it means all the back-up supports as well as the front end, one-on-one situations. When you exceed people's expectations you are using selling skills of the highest level. People do business with people they like and respect and exceeding their expectations evokes those feelings. So who can you gobsmack today?

TAKE CARE OF YOUR CUSTOMER

Success in the motor business is based on sales growth. Manufacturers build cars in large quantities so car dealers need to sell those cars in large quantities. Because when a car plant is working flat out twenty-four hours a day, the cost per car is lowest.

Every car a dealer sells should make a profit. On top of that he now has a customer for accessories, for service maintenance work, for damage repair, for new tyres and eventually for another car. If the customer stays happy he will buy another car and another car. I have a few customers each of whom has bought more than twenty cars from me over the past forty years. In fact, over a lifetime, a good customer can leave more than €250,000 in a car dealership; that's the sales volume you gain by winning and looking after one customer in the car business.

In addition, this happy customer will have family members who roll up to buy a new car. He may send work colleagues and friends to buy a car. The happier you make him, the more business referrals he will send you.

This word of mouth is the best business marketing you can invest in. So many companies spend a small fortune on advertising for new customers and will not spend anything on taking care of the customers they have. Simple mathematics shows that if you sell 400 cars a year, after three years you should have 1,200 customers. Most people change their car on a three-year cycle so in year four you have 400 customers from year one to sell to as well as trying to get a new 400. But the odds are that you will only get 100 of those original 400 customers. Why? Well, there is an amount of normal attrition because people move to a new address that's not so handy. People move up to a more prestigious brand of car or a different make for family reasons. But fifty per cent of them go somewhere else because they are not happy with the experience. That's why we need to put more resources into taking care of the customer.

This syndrome applies to most businesses. We spend big on trying to attract new customers and we don't spend enough taking good care of the customers we have. Invest in taking care of your customers and that will grow your business faster than advertising will. If you are a marketing director whose job it is to win new business make sure you convince the boss that a substantial part of the marketing budget should go into taking care of your existing customers.

NOTHING IS SOLD UNTIL IT'S PAID FOR

Even when you cut your profit margins, it's a fact of business that high sales volume will bring you high profits. But the real key to profit is the cashflow: you must get paid on the nail. It's no use making big sales if you don't get paid fast.

Cashflow is the lifeblood of every business, so when you are selling always make sure you are getting paid fast, preferably up front.

Try ordering a computer from Michael Dell. We phoned in our first order for twenty computers some years ago. When we enquired about a delivery date we were informed, 'The computers will be delivered fourteen days after your payment cheque has been cleared through our bank.' Dell gets paid in advance and has your money in his bank before he even schedules your computer to be assembled. Wow! He has millions of customer dollars to finance his business. We gave him that money because he had the best computer at the best price and he met his delivery commitments.

I used a similar plan when I took over the near-bankrupt Renault Ireland distribution company back in 1986. We had no cash but we had a debtors asset of IR£4 million that was for cars supplied to dealers on sale or return. This meant the dealers didn't pay for the car until they sold it to a customer. If they hadn't sold it in six months, they had the option of paying for the car then or returning it to us.

Now, I had purchased Renault from a very wealthy company named Waterford Crystal who could afford to have an IR£4 million debt on their balance sheet. But we needed that money paid in quick if we were to survive. So we put a finance plan in place with our bank and got the bank to pay us for the cars that the dealers had. The dealers paid the bank when the car was sold. We paid the bank the interest for the period the dealer had the car. A win-win-win situation for everyone. The dealer still got his car interest-free, the bank got some profitable business, but *we got paid the day we shipped the car.* This deal freed up IR£4 million and that cashflow helped us get up off the ground. Cash is king.

In your own business, make sure the payment terms are part of the selling process and get paid up front like Michael Dell. When you check into a hotel they swipe your credit card. When you book an airline ticket they get your credit card. All sales today should be for payment on or prior to delivery of the goods or services.

Whatever you sell, remember a golden rule Molly Darcy told me when I was selling penny apples: 'Nothing is sold until it's paid for.'

STAND OUT FROM THE CROWD

When I was selling balloons on Henry Street at Christmas time, I had a dozen different-coloured balloons flying high above my pitch on a twelve-foot long piece of string. I also drew cats' faces on the balloons with a fluorescent pen. In a throng of two hundred street sellers my balloons stood out from the crowd, or maybe flew up above the crowd.

I learned later on in a night-school marketing class that this was referred to as a unique selling proposition. My product was perceived to be better than the competition, or at least different from the others.

With our ball-game rosettes, we did the same by sticking

pictures of the team stars on the rosettes. With the dolls we sold, we put them in Judy Garland or Marilyn Monroe-style dresses. When a family bought apples, we gave the kids a few free lollipops. When I hired a wicker cart to bring my mother's fruit from the market to her stall I also did three or four runs for other traders at a fee. Which gave the Ma a price advantage because we made a profit on the deal while our competitors had the extra delivery cost. It's all about getting an advantage over the competition, preferably showing you can give added value or at least being different enough to attract customers. You will win customers when they perceive that you are better in some way than the competition. DHL and Federal Express offer faster delivery and worldwide service. Toyota say they sell the best built cars in the world. Carlsberg make what is 'probably' the best lager in the world.

Volvo once owned the word 'safety' in motor cars until two things happened. Firstly, in America they ran a television advertisement showing the giant tractor Bigfoot running over the roofs of eight cars, including a Volvo. All the roofs collapsed under the weight except the Volvo. Safety in our cars. But the authorities were tipped off that Volvo had welded iron bars inside their car to hold up the roof. They were fined hundreds of thousands of dollars, their ad agency of twenty years was fired, as were some top executives in Volvo. Reputations need always be protected with integrity.

Secondly, Renault now holds a record of seven awards for five-star safety from the independent testing organisation Euro-Ncap. That's twice as good as any other car maker in Europe and justifies Renault's slogan – The Safest Cars You Can Drive. Which is why Renault, not Volvo, now own the word 'safety' in the motor industry.

On a company or a personal basis, focus on a competitive advantage that lets you stand out from the crowd.

TEACH A MAN TO FISH

Renault Ireland have always invested in training our people. Some induction courses take place at my home in County Kildare, a peaceful country estate where we try to bond new recruits and different dealer teams together. In-house we have the Renault Training Institute, which trains our dealer people on an ongoing basis for technical competence, selling skills and people skills.

We are just about to launch a new venture, the Europa Academy, which is a €10 million investment dedicated to excellence in the automotive industry. This will add management and leadership skills to a wider curriculum. It will also bring customers from all the new EU countries who will have the advantage of training through the medium of English – and get further English lessons while with us.

Too many companies do not appreciate enough that their company grows through people. When you train and develop your own people you get the best and you get loyalty. Even when they move on, you have the satisfaction of participation in their achievements and your reputation is such that they can be replaced by eager new recruits.

I see my company role today as the teacher – the wise old guy who has been around in his business for fifty years. The one who is available to listen and give guidance and advice to my guys. The fact that I own the company lends weight to my advice but I do let them make their own mistakes. When you get burned you never stick your finger in the fire again and you grow from the failures.

I still find time to visit a few schools a month to give an hour's talk to young people. I talk about my philosophy of success and what that means to them. They all want to be millionaires, you know, until I point out that money without good health is useless.

So, when we looked at how you can learn to be lucky, I hope you noticed there was as much emphasis on the word **learn** in that chapter as there was on the word **lucky**. The more you learn, the luckier you will be. So never stop learning.

I'm still reading two books a week because, as my great friend, the Kerry poet Professor Brendan Kennelly said, 'The more I learn the more I know that what's worth learning is beyond knowledge.' Think about that one, because like Brendan I have learned the truth of what he said; and learning, learning, learning is what life is about. You will learn from books but you will remember longer the lessons you learn from your experience.

SELLING ANYTHING TO ANYONE

The selling skills you develop over the years are money in the bank. Every company needs people who can sell. It's not confined to a specific product because if you can sell one product you can sell anything. Because all the time it's you that you are selling and customers are buying into your sincerity, your integrity and the fact that you can give them what they want. Salespeople usually work on a commission basis. The more you sell, the more you are paid. So it's you yourself that puts the limit on your income. Some salespeople make more money than the boss.

The Number One car salesman in the world is Joe Girard.

He features in the *Guinness Book of Records* as having sold 1,647 new cars in one year to individual buyers. Wow! His commission cheque was nearly as much as the dealership profits. Did he go and open his own business? No. He didn't want to run a business. He wanted to stay selling cars. Meeting people was what he loved. The challenge of selling more cars each week, each month, each year was his passion. He hired two assistants to do the paperwork and follow-ups for him and paid their salaries himself. He was a business within a business and he was number one because he loved what he did and was a great sales professional. He had a passion that took him to the top.

Develop your selling skills, because that's what makes the difference when it comes to making it to the top. Joe Girard wrote a book called *How to Sell Anything to Anyone*. Put it on your list of books to learn from.

MAKE A NAME FOR YOURSELF

When you are working for a company you are working to develop the brand of the company. But you must also develop your own brand within the business. Don't just think of yourself as an employee, think of yourself as the owner and see things with the owner's eyes. That way you will always be proactive in correcting things you see wrong, instigating efforts to do things better and being available to finish a job or look after a customer. That's the way you will be noticed and you build your brand by being noticed.

I was offered a job in the famous Guinness Brewery as a messenger boy in the mid 'fifties. The personnel manager showed me the remuneration chart starting at twelve shillings a week in Year One, increasing yearly to eleven pounds a week after forty years. Plus two pints of free Guinness a day after I reached my twenty-first birthday. The personnel manager was upset when I told him it wasn't enough.

'Are you declining a position with *the* brewery?' he asked, flabbergasted, with eyebrows raised and the glasses falling off his nose.

'Yes, I'm sorry Mister, the Ma couldn't afford such a drop in my revenue stream.' The Da couldn't believe it either. He worked in Brooks Thomas for forty years to leave with a gold-plated inscribed watch and a pension of fifteen shillings a week. But the Ma understood all right.

'Don't worry about this young fella, isn't he me lucky child? He's going to make a name for himself somewhere, that's for sure.'

There's a lovely ring to that phrase. Make a name for yourself. It sums up all the guru-speak about achieving, and it was spoken by a woman whose schooling came from the streets and common sense. It's a great piece of advice because it translates into 'Build your own brand'.

My first deliberate move to make a name for myself was when I started selling cars in Walden Ford. We were given company business cards like this:

WALDEN MOTOR COMPANY

William P. J. Cullen
Junior Sales Representative

171 Parnell Street
Dublin 1   Phone 427682

That was the formal style of business cards back in those days. It was all about the company and it told anyone I gave it to that I was way down on the totem pole. So I invested in my own business cards that looked like this:

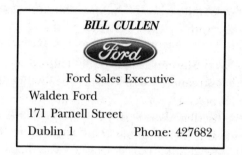

BILL CULLEN

Ford Sales Executive
Walden Ford
171 Parnell Street
Dublin 1   Phone: 427682

I scattered these around like confetti. Everyone who bought a car from me got a dozen for the pals. It appeared I was the big Ford chief based in Walden's offices in Dublin. The guy with the connections to get you the right car at the right price just when you wanted it. And I highlighted one of the best known brands in the world.

Your business card is one of the best selling tools you can use. Always carry them with you and use them to network everywhere you go. Hand one to every person you make contact with. At hotel receptions, at seminars, and conferences, at parties, in pubs, in restaurants – with a nice little message to the chef. A business card is a great networking tool because, just like a smile, every time you give one to someone, they give you one back. Develops your networking, builds your database, enhances your selling skills.

Many years ago Jackie and I used to go to a small local restaurant most Saturday nights. It was run by a hardworking girl, Rhona Teehan, who was a busy owner, chef, server, and cleaner-upper. A great girl, she has gone on to bigger and better things. But one evening in great excitement she said 'Bill, look outside the door, isn't it terrific, isn't it gorgeous?'

I looked outside and saw a brand new Ford Fiesta. I was a Ford dealer then and I asked Rhona where she had bought the car.

'I didn't know anyone in the motor business, so my flatmate brought me up to her dealership.'

Well, I wasn't giving out business cards then as much as I do now.

'Tell me, Rhona, what do you think I do for a living?' She paused, looked at my size eighteen neck, and my blue shirt and said, 'Aren't you a policeman?' I lost a deal because I wasn't scattering enough business cards. Learn from that. Everywhere you go, leave your card because **business is a two-way street**.

A PASSION FOR SERVICE

There was a time in my early career when we were taught to 'satisfy' the customer, and be 'enthusiastic' about your job. Now we know that satisfying the customer is not enough. Everyone is doing that. We now have to stand out from the crowd and 'delight' the customer. And enthusiasm is luke-warm today – we now have to be 'passionate' about our business because the other guys are getting better all the time. If you are not going forward you are going backwards because the other guy is passing you. There is no such thing as standing still.

If there's one word in the achiever's dictionary that I love, it's passion. As a matter of fact, in every Renault dealership that I own in Ireland we have twelve **Passion Banners** hanging in the showrooms. These banners are to remind our staff of why they are employed – to delight our customers. And who pays their wages? Those same customers!

The more passion they have for those priorities the more successful the dealership will be and the more successful they will be. The banners have a slogan and a picture and you can see how our customers like them too.

Passion, that's a word that conjures up all the emotions of striving, determination, achieving, loving, winning. If you can harness some of the passions on those banners, and apply them to your attitude to your business career, you will succeed beyond all your expectations. Because you know what? There are very few guys who carry those passions around with them.

Passion banners

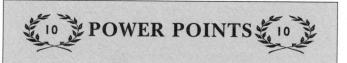

POWER POINTS

You Supercharge Your Selling Skills

- By **KNOWING WHAT YOUR CUSTOMERS WANT** – and giving it to them.

- By **HELPING PEOPLE TO BUY** and knowing that the hard sell is out.

- By **HAVING A PASSION FOR SERVICE** and knowing the customer pays your salary.

- By **EXCEEDING EXPECTATIONS** which is how to delight your customers.

- By **MAKING A NAME FOR YOURSELF** as you build your brand for the future.

- By **ALWAYS** having your **BUSINESS CARDS WITH YOU EVERYWHERE YOU GO.**

- By **PUTTING YOURSELF** in the **CUSTOMER'S SHOES.**

- By **STANDING OUT FROM THE CROWD.**

- By **LEARNING TO FISH.**

8

THE GOLDEN APPLES WAY
TO LIFETIME SUCCESS

- **THE WISDOM OF MOLLY DARCY**
- **WHAT IS LIFETIME SUCCESS?**
- **FOCUS ON ACHIEVING TODAY**
- **ATTITUDE FOR ACHIEVING**
- **YOUR POWER POINTS FOR THE JOURNEY**

THE WISDOM OF MOLLY DARCY

This grandmother of mine was a very special person. Born in a gypsy caravan she never went to any school. But she was an observer and an absorber of life patterns. She had learned from experience and by looking and listening. She also had very deep Christian beliefs and the wisdom that comes from helping people with their problems. Molly Darcy went to church at least twice a day, starting with her early morning Mass and Holy Communion. She always carried her rosary beads with her everywhere she went. In quiet moments on the street you would see her lips moving in prayer as the beads slipped slowly through her fingers.

As an altar boy I knew the Mass in Latin off by heart from 'Et Introibo Ad Altare Dei' to the last blessing. I read the lives of the famous saints and was a great fan of St Luke. I still have a dog-eared copy of *Dear And Glorious Physician*, the story of Luke, the Roman doctor, who never saw or met Jesus Christ, and his gospel was bedtime reading for me in my teenage years.

While I fell away from religious discipline in my thirties, I never changed my habits of quiet meditation. I have never forgotten Molly Darcy's teachings: that we all have a purpose for living on this earth. Molly said the purpose of life is to know and serve Jesus Christ by helping others. I have fine-tuned my belief that our purpose in life is to use our God-given talents to their fullest potential.

WHAT IS LIFETIME SUCCESS?

You first have to identify what success means to you and I hope you know that now from the use of your **Wheel of Lifetime Success**. You should get organised to have your daily action steps that will fast track your continued improvement that will lead you to achieve your successes.

I have always found that achievement of any goal, no matter how small, gave me a great sense of physical and spiritual exhilaration. Scoring a goal in a football match, hitting a sales target, exceeding a charity fund-raising objective, finalising a good business deal, all gave me an endorphin-rush, the happy chappies visit. Small achievements will lead you to the bigger goals and that's the path to growing as a person. It's these small achievements which fuel your desire to be the best you can be. They will bring you to realise the amazing potential you have to be a really terrific person. This growth as a person is the core of endless energy. As you discard your negative baggage by developing more and more success habits you will be revitalised.

How you use your time will dictate your achievements in life. That's the principle of **Lifetime Success**. It's so important to be in control of your time. How often have you said 'I don't have time to do that' or, 'I ran out of time today' or, 'There's no time to wait' or, 'Where would I get time for that?' Use the time audit to get yourself a bundle of extra time – but make sure you use that time for action steps to develop your success habits.

FOCUS ON ACHIEVING TODAY

Smile and the world smiles with you. Really believe in the wonderful potential you have to achieve any realistic goal and then really, really, really focus on achieving – today. Find the time for yourself every day to complete some action steps, and always stay in your **Today Zone**. Don't waste time daydreaming about yesterday or into the future. Positive actions today will make your tomorrow the future that you are dreaming about.

Make sure health and happiness are your primary goals. That *you* come first and family is your most important core value. As you achieve your action steps you will grow in confidence, which will push you to aim higher and achieve more. You will grow as your potential unfolds and expands. Your energy will multiply as our fitness plan takes effect.

You will attract good luck as you develop your success habits. Build those good habits of respect for others particularly parents, teachers and older people. The habit of being generous and supportive. Of helping people especially those in need and less well off. The habit of learning and the habit of loving. The more you give to others the greater the gifts you will receive, and the more good luck will come your way. You can start all this today!

Over the last six chapters, you have read my **Six Simple Steps to Success**. The habits you can develop will multiply your opportunities to achieve, to realise your potential and make your dreams come true. It works for me, and when you look at the lives of any great achiever you will see that they all possessed these core abilities. So let's just recap on what I've learned from sixty years of experience, and first let's recall the wisdom of Molly Darcy.

ATTITUDE FOR ACHIEVING

ATTITUDE is the most important factor in achieving. Having a positive attitude and believing you can make it happen. Stay far away from all negative influences. Visualise yourself with your goals achieved. Dress and look and feel confident. Use the affirmation 'I am terrific' and never leave your home without a smile on your face. Make sure you have a hero whose qualities you admire.

YOUR POWER POINTS FOR THE JOURNEY

PLAN OF ACTION

The key chapter is your **PLAN OF ACTION**. You can read this book today and guess what? Like the people who journey to the gym in New Year, the dieters who commit to losing weight, the smokers who decide to quit, you can forget about it all in a few days. You have to write your plan of actions now. **Do it now**. Get your planner out, or buy a planner or get out some sheets of paper **right now**. It's a simple exercise as shown in Chapter 3 but I want to repeat it again.

PEOPLE SKILLS

PEOPLE is what life is all about and improving your people skills will accelerate your success. Learn to be a good conversationalist by listening. When you make people feel special they will want to help you. Give customers a happy experience and they will become customers for life. You can develop your leadership skills and learn how to get people to want to help you.

LEARN TO BE LUCKY

Yes, you can learn to be **LUCKY**. It's about learning to become an expert at what you want to do. It's about making yourself available with all those abilities and skills you've learned. It's about doing it better than the other guy and having the confidence in yourself to create opportunities. And when you do unto others you will always be lucky.

ENERGY TO EXCEL

ENERGY is the force of life, of health, of achieving. You get energy from eating the right food, drinking the right drinks, and you kill energy with alcohol, junk food, drugs and cigarettes. You treble your energy with exercise, and a daily workout is the foundation of great health. The Golden Apples Fitness Plan will make you energised and dynamic. Vitamins will give you longevity and a disease-free life. Make sure you use every God-given minute to enjoy your potential to achieve.

SELL WITH A SMILE

SELLING SKILLS should be taught in schools. You need to realise that selling is really helping people to buy. The easy way to do that is to know what the customers want – a happy, hassle-free experience, a cool product, a service that exceeds expectations. You have to deliver your brand by making a name for yourself, and having a passion for taking care of people.

Your **Plan of Action** is your roadmap to success. To achieve your goals you must:

- Write down your **ten core values** and identify your **goals**.

- Use the **Wheel of Lifetime** to develop your plan of action.

- Use the **Power of Ten** to stay on the road to continuous improvement.

- Realise that how you use your **time** will dictate your achievements in life.

- Get some **Action Steps** done every day, without fail, no excuses.

- Don't procrastinate, every journey starts with the first step so **do it now!**

9

INSPIRATIONS
FOR YOUR JOURNEY

- JOHN B. KEANE
- HENRY FORD
- SIR RICHARD BRANSON
- SIR STANLEY MATTHEWS
- NELSON MANDELA
- DALEY THOMPSON
- MICHAEL FLATLEY

Consider these outstanding achievers and let them inspire you on your journey to success.

JOHN B. KEANE

Our late, great, Kerry playwright John B. Keane wrote many wonderful plays and is most famous for *The Field* which became a big screen hit starring the Irish actor Richard Harris.

We'd meet John B. on occasion in the Kingdom of Kerry and he was particularly taken by my stories of the courage of my mother in the face of deprivation and adversity. He encouraged me to write the story of my Dublin childhood and the vanished community in which I was raised. He said it was a story of family that our children's children should know.

John B. Keane

Richard Harris

'The women of Ireland,' he said, 'were the backbone of the Irish nation and you have to tell the story of that amazing mother of yours. She had more lee-a-roady* than any man, so write the book **now**. Do it now because

> *Bones Don't Speak*
> *And Dust Is Silent Too!'*

John B. had cancer when he spoke those words, which impacted so much on me that I sat down and wrote the chapter outline of *Penny Apples* that evening. I finished the book in time to read some excerpts at his Listowel Writers' Festival in 2002 on the day he was buried. Thank you, John B., for your inspirational reminder that we are only passing through.

DO IT NOW!

* lee-a-roady is Gaelic for 'Balls'

Henry Ford

HENRY FORD

Way back in 1847, at age twenty-one, William Ford left the desolation of his home in Ballenascarthy, County Cork to escape the famine plague that was devastating Ireland. William and the Ford family set out from Cobh just outside Cork City on the ship to America. Thomasina Ford, his mother, died of cholera on the journey and was buried at sea.

The family settled in Dearborn, Michigan, where young William Ford married Mary Litogot in April 1861 and their son Henry Ford was born in July 1863.

So the son of a poor Irish farmer who escaped the great famine became the founder of the Ford global empire. Today Ford Motor Corporation is one of the world's Top

Ten Companies, and the Ford Charity Foundation has assets of $13 billion, and gives $1 billion a year to deserving causes worldwide. William Clay Ford, the namesake of his great, great grandfather, is President of that empire today.

Henry Ford has been credited with many inspirational sayings. The one I remember best is the one you must keep in your heart.

> 'Whether You Believe You Can
> Or You Can't – You're Right'

SIR RICHARD BRANSON

He is famous worldwide for his Virgin brand, for his music megastores, his international airline, plus 200 companies in over thirty countries. He is a billionaire who lives life to the full, in his dramatic high speed Atlantic boat crossings, and his record-breaking balloon trips across the Atlantic and Pacific Oceans. This man epitomises the word entrepreneur – he is the ultimate risk taker. A happy, healthy achiever!

Richard Branson's business career started while he was still at school, when he established a national magazine entitled *Student* at the age of sixteen. That was his first step on the journey to make his dreams come true. Today, we call him the six billion dollar man as his annual company revenues have reached that figure. At a youthful fifty-three years old, he has the energy and ability to push his envelope of achievements to new heights. You could join him on his Virgin Spaceship One for a take-off to the stratosphere.

SIR STANLEY MATTHEWS

One of my great sporting heroes of all times is the late Sir Stanley Matthews. He was the first footballer to be made a Knight of the Realm, a quiet man who played for England's international soccer team and won fifty-four caps for his country. He was a non-drinking, non-smoking fitness expert who kept himself in great shape and played for Stoke City in the English First Division, then the Premier Division of that era.

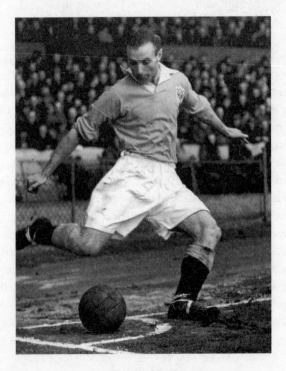

Sir Stanley Matthews

Sir Stanley played his last game in the first team jersey at fifty years old. Yes, he had the young twenty year olds chasing after him, unable to get the ball from him, and he a grandad! He was never sent off in any football game and in fact was never booked once in his thirty-four years in soccer. Fit as a fiddle he was, and lived on until he was eighty-four years old.

My Da used to say, 'Matthews is the greatest soccer player of all time – you wanna be top class, son, you just copy his habits. No booze, no cigarettes, and exercise every day.' It certainly motivated me and helped fashion my approach to evolving the lifestyle of a happy, healthy achiever!

NELSON MANDELA

Whenever you are feeling low, under stress, or thinking poor old me, just look at the picture on page 190. Cut it out and put it on the wall where you'll see it every day. Why?

This is Nelson Mandela who spent thirty years in a dark prison cell in the notorious Robben Island Prison on a small island off the coast of Africa. But Mandela never did self-pity – his courage and his dignity persevered through all those years. He not only survived this deprivation – he grew stronger!

He always has a smile on his face and he epitomises the A-P-P-L-E-S philosophy I have set out in this book. In that dark prison he ingrained his life habits:

Up at 4.30 a.m. every day
Exercise for one hour every day
Disciplined eating has given him longevity (he is eighty-six)
He updates his goals every week
His time management is famous

Nelson Mandela, whose courage and resilience
are an example to all of us

He works twelve hours every day
He travels the world

Nelson Mandela is admired and respected worldwide
as a great man, a statesman, an achiever. He is a Nobel Peace
Prize recipient and his life is an inspiration to all of us.

DALEY THOMPSON

Daley Thompson is a man of iron, having won the Olympic
Decathlon gold twice – as a twenty-year-old youth in Moscow
1980 and in Los Angeles 1984, setting an Olympic and world
record for this punishing event.

Daley Thompson

The Decathlon athlete has to be world class in ten events: he needs strength for the shot-put and discus, speed for the sprints, endurance for the 1500 metres, flexibility and power for the jumps and pole vaults, stamina and determination to compete in ten events over four days. Daley held the world, and European records – a unique achievement.

Daley is an extrovert who brought colour and charisma to

191

the athletic world. He proved what you can achieve by persistence and dedication – and always believing he was the best in the world!

I had the privilege of walking the thirty-two mile Channel Tunnel from France to England with him, and his people skills encouraged everyone to the finish line. A happy healthy high achiever!

MICHAEL FLATLEY

Michael Flatley is a man who has achieved global fame through sheer determination and belief in himself. From

Michael Flatley

Dancing Champion of the World

his earliest days in Chicago he showed relentless focus – winning a Golden Gloves boxing championship at seventeen years old.

But his dream was to be the greatest dancer in the world. He wrote it down; he practised, practised, practised. He drew inspiration from his mother and grandmother – both champion Irish dancers who encouraged his ambitions. To this day Michael leaves a front row seat empty at all his shows to remind him that his Irish grandmother is still there encouraging him to be the best.

Michael Flatley as a boxer could have been a world champion. Michael Flatley as an Irish dancer was the world champion. Michael Flatley as a flute player was the All Ireland Champion. At thirty years old he had achieved the Master of Dance Award and became the youngest person ever to be awarded the National Heritage Awards from President Ronald Reagan, confirming his place as one of America's greatest living artistes.

But the best was yet to come. In 1994, in Dublin, Michael presented the first *Riverdance* show – a five-minute warmer-up to the Eurovision Song Contest that brought the house down. A magical performance that has seen *Riverdance* go round the world over the last ten years.

But a shareholding dispute saw Michael leave the show to focus on his own dream, his 100 per cent ownership of a new production – *Lord Of The Dance*, which at the Academy Awards of 1996 amazed 2.5 billion people worldwide. He then brought *Feet Of Flame* to the stage and these two shows earn Michael millions of dollars a week.

He has broken his own world tap dancing record by hitting thirty-five taps per second. But he still credits his success to his positive belief in himself. On his opening night at the London Coliseum he defied the doctor's instructions for a six-week layout and bandaged his torn calf muscle before dancing through the pain to give a magnificent performance.

'Nothing can stop me. I trick my mind into believing I can do it. Everything is positive. I don't let negative energy into my life.'

At forty-six years old, Michael Flatley is an example of tremendous determination, resilience, discipline and lee-a-roady.

10

THE IRISH ACHIEVERS

- **THE THREE AMIGOS**
- **MICHAEL SMURFIT**
- **SIR ANTHONY O'REILLY**
- **SEAN FITZPATRICK**
- **PADDY KELLY**
- **THE RYANAIR STORY**

THE THREE AMIGOS

Having started my career selling apples on the streets of Dublin, it's no wonder I called my autobiography *It's A Long Way From Penny Apples*. Here I am now in the luxury of the world famous Sandy Lane Resort in Barbados putting the final touches to this book. Only a week after Tiger Woods took over the resort for his wedding.

Writing about achievement prompted me to recognise a trio of Ireland's greatest achievers, the owners of Sandy

J.P. McManus, John Magnier and Dermot Desmond

Lane: Dermot Desmond and J.P. McManus. With their great friend John Magnier, they have taken the world by storm. From humble origins they have amassed a business empire from Ireland to England to America and Europe.

Dermot Desmond's career started as an accountant with Coopers & Lybrand and he went on to open his own stockbroking and investment business in the early 'eighties. The economy in Ireland was suffering badly then, and Dermot with it. But in 1987 the Irish Taoiseach, Charlie Haughey, supported Dermot's plan to build an Irish financial services centre in Dublin's docklands with tax incentives for in-coming investment. It was a huge success and this project was the kick-start for the Celtic Tiger and Dermot's empire.

His investment in the Glagow Celtic soccer club and his purchase of London City airport is on the way to making him another fortune. His shrewd financial brain and his willingness to go against the tide have propelled him to billionaire status. Never a man to forget his roots, he still has the common touch. And he's only in his early fifties now, so I feel the best of Dermot Desmond is yet to come.

J.P. McManus, Dermot's partner in many investments including Sandy Lane, is simply a phenomenon. Even in school he worked as a bookies' runner, and had the brain of a streetwise computer. The always smiling cherubic young-ster went into the bookmaking business where he went bust twice. They were two major steps on his way to success. 'When you're broke, you learn to respect money and never want to go back there again. You become stronger, wiser and more determined to succeed.' His bookmaking career went on fast-track and became the springboard into cur-rency market hedging and options, where he says a similar structure to horseracing betting exists.

Today, J.P. has his financial headquarters in Geneva and his horses at his Kilmallock Stud in his native Limerick. He has amassed a fortune of hundreds of millions but J.P. is still the smiling genial Irishman. A golfing pal of Tiger Woods, a major shareholder in Manchester United plc, this guy is one of nature's gentlemen. And his support of charitable causes is renowned – never forget your roots.

John Magnier is the quiet, retiring member of this Irish trio. The owner of Coolmore Stud is the most successful horse breeder in Ireland with his current Epsom and Irish Derby winner Galileo. His shrewd investment in thoroughbred racehorses has brought him a lavish lifestyle with homes in Tipperary, Marbella and Barbados. Like Dermot and J.P., he's always to the front in supporting charities and with J.P. he holds a big shareholding in Manchester United.

These three men reflect the success of the Celtic Tiger. In fact, they have been part of the creation of the Celtic Tiger. They enjoy financial success without any airs and graces, and are role models for the next generation of young Irish people. They have seen tough times, they have fought through the tough times, and they illustrate Kipling's words that success and failure are two sides of the same coin.

MICHAEL SMURFIT

Michael Smurfit, Chairman of Jefferson Smurfit Group plc, took his father's small Irish cardboard box company and built it into the world's largest paper packaging company employing at its peak 72,000 people. It has total managed sales, internal and external, of nearly US$20 billion per annum and operating from over 600 factories worldwide

Michael Smurfit shows Tiger Woods and Mark O'Meara some Irish hospitality at the K Club, venue for Ryder Cup 2006.

stretching from Argentina to Norway and from China to the USA.

Chairman Michael made himself a billionaire in that forty-five-year journey with luxury homes in Marbella and Monte Carlo where he is the Irish Consul General to Monaco. He developed the Kildare Hotel and Country Club into the world-renowned 'K' Club, which is the first Irish venue ever for the Ryder Cup in 2006. In the horse-racing world he set new standards when his horse Vintage Crop won the 1993 Melbourne Cup and the Irish St Leger in 1993 and 1994 – the first Irish horse to surpass £1 million in winnings.

Michael epitomises the ethos of Golden Apples. He has the lee-a-roady to take risks, he plans his actions, and he is a positive thinker. He uses his time to the full as he travels five continents building his empire. He is a happy high achiever and is one of Ireland's top philanthropists.

SIR ANTHONY O'REILLY

Tony O'Reilly is an Irish icon and one of the world's premier business leaders. He played International Rugby for Ireland at age seventeen, going on to win twenty-nine caps for his country and played for the Lions and the Barbarians. His scoring records are still unbroken to this day.

His business career took him to work as a young man in the UK for Heinz Corporation. His people skills, his attitude for achieving and his dynamic energy won him the position of CEO for Heinz Worldwide. He steered Heinz from a market capitalisation of $900 million to $15 billion on his retirement in 1998 and set an unprecedented record of twenty-two per cent shareholder growth every year for 20 years. His stock options and personal investments have

Sir Anthony O'Reilly

given him billionaire status. Retired from Heinz, he is Chief Executive and the major shareholder in Independent News & Media plc., Eircom plc., and also Waterford Wedgwood plc., with numerous other business interests. He was knighted in 2001 by Queen Elizabeth for his consistent work over twenty-five years for peace in Northern Ireland.

Sir Anthony O'Reilly's charity giving is renowned and he was a founder of the Ireland Fund that has raised US$200 million dollars for Irish charities since inception. His career is an inspiration to every achiever.

SEAN FITZPATRICK

In 1986 Anglo Irish Bank was a small Dublin Bank with a market capitalisation of €5 million when Sean Fitzpatrick took over responsibility for growing the business.

Sean Fitzpatrick

Sean had all the Golden Apples attributes and his positive attitude, self-belief, energy, and people skills, drove the bank's turnover through the roof with the lowest rate of bad debt of any bank in Europe. Sean had an entrepreneurial instinct unlike that of most bank conservatives. He backed people he believed in, and he anticipated the Irish property boom before his competitors. Anglo has one of the biggest portfolios of property developer clients in the country. Sean Fitzpatrick was the recipient of the Man of the Year Award 2004 from the Irish Chambers of Commerce, USA.

Anglo Irish today have a market capitalisation of €6.8 billion and is the fastest growing bank in Ireland thanks to the driving force of Sean Fitzpatrick.

PADDY KELLY

I first met Paddy Kelly in the early 'seventies when he was a young man building a house in the Glasnevin suburbs of North Dublin. He bought a new car from me to go on honeymoon with his new bride, Maureen.

Paddy was always in good humour, always an optimist and became a very wealthy builder developer, living in Dublin's top address at Shrewsbury Road. He had a brush with disaster as a Lloyd's Name in the 'eighties but his resilience and determination got him safely through.

Today he is at the core of many multi-million property deals in Ireland and England, and is about to commence a billion-dollar marina development on the west coast of Florida. Paddy Kelly has an amazing attitude for achievement with exceptional people skills and a smile that would charm the birds off the trees.

Paddy Kelly, 2004

All the people in these success stories have maximised their potential. They made their dreams come true. Every one of them used this Golden Apples philosophy.

Every one of them was lucky, wasn't he? Well, you can be very sure they made their own luck, the same way they generate the energy to excel – by persistence, and focused determination. They use a positive attitude to plan their action lists and maximise their time control. They are all persuasive salespeople with terrific people skills and self-belief.

Most of all they had the lee-a-roady to take risks and make extraordinary commitment on the road of achievement.

THE RYANAIR STORY

Starting as a small Irish airline in the mid eighties with two turboprop aircraft, Ryanair was treated as a cheeky upstart by the national carriers. After a rocky start, the arrival of Michael O'Leary as CEO transformed Ryanair into what is one of the largest and most profitable airlines in Europe. It now operates sixty-five Boeing 737s with 150 more aircraft on order. It blazed a trail as the low fares airline and now has a market capitalisation of five billion dollars.

O'Leary is the driving force behind Ryanair's success. His template of multi-tasking staff, fast turnaround of aircraft and no frills service has taken his passenger levels to twenty-seven million in 2004. His strategy has been copied throughout the industry but none has come close to matching his

Michael O'Leary

success. O'Leary's passion for achievement and ruthless drive to cut costs are legendary. His ambition to make Ryanair the world's largest and most profitable airline is an achievable one for this extraordinary young man – who now has a personal net worth of more than five hundred million dollars.

It should be remembered that the founder and chairman of Ryanair is Tony Ryan, who started his career in Aer Lingus before he set up Guinness Peat Aviation. He built GPA into the biggest aircraft leasing company in the world with a value of US$2 billion. His plan to take GPA public was ill-timed and was eventually taken over by GE Capital.

Tony Ryan didn't let that setback stop him from developing the Ryanair success story. In his magnificent home at Lyons Demesne outside Dublin, he is a lionheart of Irish achievers.

Dr Tony Ryan

11

CAPTURE THE VISION

- **MAKE YOUR DREAMS COME TRUE**
- **SOME PEOPLE MAY WANT OUT**
- **HOW WE CAN HELP YOU IN THE FUTURE**
- **BE A HAPPY HEALTHY ACHIEVER**

MAKE YOUR DREAMS COME TRUE

I have always had dreams. As one of fourteen kids I dreamed of having a room of my own with my own bed and my own books to read. In my teens I dreamed of having my own car. On the night John Fitzgerald Kennedy died I was a grown man of twenty-one years old. That's when my dreams turned into a vision.

Kennedy had visited Ireland just six months before he was shot. His speech to the Irish people was inspirational and his quotation from George Bernard Shaw ignited my dreams into a vision. He said:

'Some people see things and say "Why?" Other people dream things and say "Why Not?" '

That night I wrote my first dream list and I had gone way beyond beds, books and cars. I went to sleep dreaming of a business empire, a mansion, a fleet of cars, a helicopter, and an aeroplane. All the trappings of wealth and success.

But still there was the fruit stall, the fish market, and the street sellers. Never forget your roots, the Ma was whispering to me, with Molly Darcy smiling quietly beside her. The vision was so powerful, it felt real. I saw myself in the fancy office, driving the Rolls Royce, sitting in the helicopter. The happy chappies were pulsing through me. If the great-grandson of a poor Irish immigrant could become the President of the United States of America, then why couldn't I achieve my little list? That night I pledged to capture the vision. The 22nd of November, 1963.

Did I really, really, think I could do it? Forty years later, it's hard to say. But I do remember writing down my mother's words:

It's Never a Tragedy to Try Something and Fail
The Real Tragedy is Not to Try

You have your dreams just like I did. Well, if you really want to make your dreams come true, you now have a blueprint to work to. I had to figure it out for myself but you now have the benefit of all my experiences. You also have the benefit of the advice and example I had from my mentors. So you are now well ahead of the posse.

You can take my *Golden Apples* and put all that expertise to work for you. You can use my **Six Simple Steps to Success** to build your plan for the future, to capture your vision. You can now create your own future with a blueprint that works. A blueprint that has been honed and fine-tuned over sixty years of trial and error. A blueprint that is simple to adapt, simple to operate, simple to remember, simple to focus on.

Yes, you will have to make some sacrifices – but anything worth having doesn't come easy. Yes, you are going to become more disciplined – but discipline is the way of the warrior, the path to strength and success. I can only show you the way, and encourage you to keep moving on the journey of continuous improvement. You have already done the hard bit. The journey of a thousand miles starts with the first step and you have taken that first step by reading this book. The first step to becoming the person you want to be. The first step to releasing the enormous potential for achieving that's lying dormant inside you. It's now up to you to make your dreams come true.

SOME PEOPLE MAY WANT OUT

In the hustle and bustle of today's world some people want out. Away from the hassle, the stress, the unnatural world of busy, busy, busy, that we live in.

If that's how you feel, if that's what you want to do, then that's okay. Everyone has the freedom to make that choice. If you want to work in a seaside resort, a good waitress can make enough in tips to take her through the winter. If you want to live a simple lifestyle in an inexpensive rural area there's always a job to cover the low cost of living.

Maybe life has battered you too much and a slower pace without stress would be best for you. So go do that, but you should still take your **A-P-P-L-E-S** with you. You'll still have goals, you'll still need a plan of action and the energy to enjoy your new lifestyle. And no matter where you are or what you're doing a little luck always comes in handy. You can duck or dive into my **A-P-P-L-E-S** and use whatever parts you want to take on board. In its totality it might not be for everyone. But in all its guidance, there is advice and inspiration from experienced mentors that will be of help no matter where you are or what you want to do. If you do want out, make sure you take some spirituality with you.

HOW WE CAN HELP YOU IN THE FUTURE

I AM TERRIFIC

GOLDEN APPLES®
Pocket Planner

Ten out of Ten is the best you can be. Every day someone raises the bar higher, so if you are standing still the other guy is going past you. Use your action slips daily to stay on the path of continuous improvement.

LIFETIME SUCCESS
HOW YOUR TIME WILL DICTATE
YOUR LIFE ACHIEVEMENTS

Bill Cullen

Priority Action List

1. Daily Fitness Plan

2. Energising Body Scrub

3. Power Juice

4. Health Vitz

5. Energy Vitz

6. Make Someone Feel Special

7. Action Steps

BE A HAPPY HEALTHY ACHIEVER

Bill Cullen has proved that he knows what it takes to be a happy healthy achiever. He has worn the T-shirt of poverty and deprivation. He started from the very bottom of the ladder and now enjoys an extraordinary life of luxury and privilege. He has proved that we all have unlimited potential within us. His **Six Simple Steps To Success** will expand your horizons and lets you write your own roadmap to the successes you want.

To help you embrace Bill's **GOLDEN APPLES** philosophy and make it a daily part of your life, visit his website at *www.goldenapples.ie* or contact Bill at:

> Bill Cullen
> Lifetime Success Institute
> Europa Academy
> Swords
> County Dublin
> Ireland

> Fax No.:   00.353.1.870 8800
> Email: bill@goldenapples.ie
> Website: www.goldenapples.ie

where you can get Bill's pocket planner entitled *The Golden Apples Way To Lifetime Success*

This pocket planner will make the **Six Simple Steps To Success** a part of your daily life.

- It lets you carry your plan of actions with you
- It helps you revise your positive attitude daily
- It helps you focus on your priorities
- It helps you meet your commitments
- It will enhance your spirit and your energy
- It will help you to make your dreams come true

With this slim easy to use pocket planner come **Priority Action Lists** and **Steps To Success Lists** that will push you to peak performance through every day of the rest of your life.

BIBLIOGRAPHY

The Seven Habits Of Highly Effective People, Stephen Covey
First Things First, Stephen Covey
Boundless Energy, Deepak Chopra
Synchro Destiny, Deepak Chopra
The Seven Spiritual Laws of Success, Deepak Chopra
How To Win, Denis Waitley
Seeds of Greatness, Denis Waitley
WOW Projects, Tom Peters
The Art of Selling, Tom Hopkins
Natural Energy, Erika Schwartz & Carol Colman
The Brand Called You, Peter Montoya & Tim Vandehey
How To Sell Anything To Anyone, Joe Girard
Can You Manage?, Ivor Kenny
Superself, Charles Givens
How To Become A Rainmaker, Jeffrey Fox
It's Not About The Bike, Lance Armstrong
Fierce Conversations, Susan Scott
The Millionaire Next Door, Thomas Stanley & William Danko
Natural Highs, Patrick Holford & Dr Hyla Cass
Shed 10 Years In 10 Weeks, Julian Whittaker & Carol Colman
Sales Superstars, David Forward
Million Dollar Habits, Brian Tracy
The Luck Factor, Richard Wiseman
Tactics Of Very Successful People, Eugene Griesman
The Tipping Point, Malcolm Gladwell
Energy Forever, Sid Kurchheimer & Gale Malesky
Follow This Path, Curt Coffman & Gabriel Gonzalez-Molina
The Ultimate Ace Diet, Janette Marshall
How To Make People Like You, Nicholas Boothman
It's Not Luck, Eliyahu Goldratt
Selling To Win, Richard Denny
Lions Don't Need To Roar, D.A. Benton
The Official Guide To Success, Tom Hopkins
What Clients Love, Harry Beckwith

INDEX

PICTURE
ACKNOWLEDGEMENTS

The author and publisher are grateful to the following for permission to use copyright material

page vii   The Ma, Molly Darcy, the Da – Family Archive
page xviii   Bill Cullen – Andy Murray and © Andy Murray
Page 1   Map of Dublin – Reproduced with kind permission of Collins Maps & Atlases
Page 2   Bill's mother (Mary Darcy) etc. – Family Archive
Page 9   Selling the fruit and vegetables etc. – Family Archive
Page 35   Lance Armstrong – © Martin Bureau/AFG/Getty Images
Page 36   Kelly Holms – Courtesy of Independent Newspapers Ireland Ltd
Page 37   Bill and the helicopter – Family Archives
Page 52   Cian O'Connor – Courtesy of Independent Newspapers Ireland Ltd
Page 61   Suggested Core Values – Designed by Bill Cullen and © Bill Cullen
Page 62   Suggested Focus Points – Designed by Bill Cullen and © Bill Cullen
Page 63   Make Your Own Wheel – Designed by Bill Cullen and © Bill Cullen
Page 65   Muhammad Ali & Sonny Liston – © John Pineda/Getty Images Sport/Getty Images
Page 79   Smiling Cat – Anonymous
Page 88   Selling Balloons – Family Archive
Page 90   Molly Darcy pictures – Family Archive
Pages 98–99   'I Whistle a Happy Tune' © Richard Rodgers & Osean Hammerstein's II Courtesy R and H WIllianson Music © EMI
Page 125   Flexibility Warm Up – Designed by Bill Cullen and © Bill Cullen